INDIAN SUMMER

Printed in the United States of America
Rodale Inc. makes every effort to use acid-free ∞, recycled paper ♻.

Book design by Christopher Rhoads

Library of Congress Cataloging-in-Publication Data

McDonald, Brian.
    Indian summer : the forgotten story of Louis Sockalexis, the first
Native American in major league baseball / Brian McDonald.
        p.   cm.
    ISBN 1–57954–587–4 hardcover
    1. Sockalexis, Louis, 1871–1913.   2. Baseball players—United
States—Biography.   3. Indian baseball players—Biography.   I. Title.
GV865.S588 M33   2003
796.357'092—dc21   2002153791

Distributed to the book trade by St. Martin's Press

2   4   6   8   10   9   7   5   3   1   hardcover

Visit us on the Web at www.rodalestore.com, or call us toll-free at (800) 848-4735.

WE INSPIRE AND ENABLE PEOPLE TO IMPROVE
THEIR LIVES AND THE WORLD AROUND THEM

INDIAN SUMMER

BRIAN McDONALD

THE FORGOTTEN STORY OF LOUIS SOCKALEXIS THE FIRST NATIVE AMERICAN IN MAJOR LEAGUE BASEBALL

RODALE

For Dad

PROLOGUE

Legend has it that on the night before Christmas Eve, 1913, a Penobscot Indian logger named Louis Francis Sockalexis sat on the bank of a frozen stream and gazed up at the black sky. Slow-moving clouds began to cover the moon, dimming its borrowed light. Snow crunched beneath the footfalls of an approaching fellow logger. Sockalexis did not turn to greet his visitor, but rather kept his eyes fixed on the darkening sphere. "The moon is going to rest," Sockalexis said, "and so soon will I."

The following evening the loggers were called in for dinner by the clang of a cast-iron bar, which echoed incongruously through the silent Maine forest. Snow fell softly on the shoulders of the workers as they trudged their way back to the communal cabin. There someone noticed that the Chief, as they called him, was missing. Several of the loggers pulled on their coats and went in search of him. They found Sockalexis lying next to a half-axed pine; his face, flabby and creased from years of drinking cheap booze, was dusted with snow. The Indian's brave heart had given out with his last swing of the axe. Back at the cabin a logger removed Sockalexis's coat, then his heavy woolen sweater. The others

gathered close as their coworker peeled off the first of many yel-
lowed newspaper clippings that the Chief had kept hidden beneath
his clothing.

In his book *They Played the Game*, Harry Grayson calls Louis
Sockalexis baseball's most tragic figure. Blessed with Olympic
sprinter speed, an arm like a Winchester rifle, and a penchant for
the dramatic game-winning hit or catch, Sockalexis had the talent
to be the best-known baseball player of his era. Indeed, for many
years after Sockalexis died, those who had watched him play lined
up to tell the world how good he was. When asked about
Sockalexis, Bill "Rough" Carrigan, the manager of the old-time
Boston Red Sox, said: "I don't remember ever seeing a quicker bat
or a stronger arm. . . . Possibly the one player worthy of a com-
parison is that young man, Joe DiMaggio. He has a trace of
Sockalexis's stuff, but I don't believe he can run or throw with the
Indian." Hughie Jennings, longtime Detroit Tigers manager, went
one better: "At no time has a player crowded so many remarkable
accomplishments into such a short period. He should have been the
greatest player of all time—greater than Cobb, Wagner, Lajoie,
Hornsby, and any of the other men who made history for the game
of baseball." While managing the New York Giants in the National
League from 1902 to 1932, John McGraw would often talk about
his time playing against "the Indian."

For one short season, Sockalexis played the game like no one
had before and very few have since. But pressure collapsed into

weakness. In what has become an all-too-familiar scenario with sports stars today, he flushed his talent away in a river of alcohol and, in doing so, inflated the stereotype that haunted him throughout his career. His predilection for booze, however, was only part of the story.

Although baseball historians place James Madison Troy, who played in the American Association in 1887 and 1890, as the first American Indian professional ballplayer, Troy played without acknowledging his race. Sockalexis not only acknowledged his race but saw it plastered all over sports pages throughout the country. He came to professional baseball at a time when the Indian wars were still fresh in the minds of the American people. Because of his proximity to arguably this country's defining moment, the conquering of the Western frontier, he was a national news story before he stepped on his first major league field. He seemed well equipped for the challenge. Besides his undeniable talent, he was good looking, college educated, and immensely likable.

In many ways, Sockalexis mirrored the twenty-seven-year-old Dodger rookie who would break baseball's color barrier fifty years after him. But unlike Jackie Robinson, Sockalexis has not yet been granted such an illustrious place in history—partly because the Indian nation has been shattered and the pieces swept into remote corners of this country called reservations. American Indians then were thought of in a kind of clownish revisionism. While Sockalexis dazzled the National League, Buffalo Bill Cody's Wild West Show with its "Injun warriors" played to sold-out crowds in venues across the country. Despite this overwhelmingly pitiful backdrop to his story, Sockalexis lived and played heroically and with a kind of sublime innocence.

For me, this morphing of man and myth presented something of a quandary. I started this project believing that I could separate the two. I couldn't. The way American society viewed Sockalexis says as much about his life and times as does documented fact. I also acknowledge that here and there I take literary license—I fill in some blanks. But I make these assumptions having done exhaustive research. I must say, for me the best part of this project was the research. Much like the loggers who surrounded his body, as I peeled back one news clipping after another about his career, there could be no doubt: The old Indian had once been professional baseball's biggest sensation.

ouldn't Concede a Boston College Touchdown—Boston, 8; Holy Cross, 6.

The spectators at the South end rounds yesterday afternoon were treated to a mixture of foot ball, scrapping and poor decisions. Holy Cross played what is commonly called a "dirty" game, and Dadmun, alternately referee and umpire, made numerous bad decisions, always against Boston College. Dadmun's work was hissed and hooted by the large contingent from both colleges. In striking contrast to the work of Holy Cross was the clean and earnest game out up by Boston College.

The field was in a deplorable condition, the southerly end being a stretch of mud and slush. The playing under the circumstances was remarkably good.

Boston lost the toss and was given the ball, with the wind against her. Lyons kicked out of bounds twice and the ball went to Holy Cross. Kenney then kicked off to Vahey on the 15-yard line and he advanced the ball 10 yards. White gained three yards around the right end, and then Boston lost on downs. The ball was regained by Boston on a fumble, but lost again on downs. Holy Cross fumbled once more, and Boston put McGrath through centre for three yards. Long was hurt on the next play.

When the game was resumed the ball was passed to White, who started for right end. Sockalexis broke through and tackled White, who had already passed the ball to Croker, who, aided by splendid interference, circled the end for 80 yards. It was a pretty criss-cross and evoked a storm of applause. Landrigan was then pushed over the line on the next play. Lyon failed to kick goal.

In the second half Boston's line failed to hold, and by successive mass plays Holy Cross carried the ball over for a touchdown. The ball was punted out, and caught by Campbell one foot from the side line. Linehan then kicked an almost impossible goal, and the crowd cheered. It was a feat to be proud of.

Sockalexis, the Indian, played at halfback for Holy Cross and he astonished the spectators by his ability. In many respects he was similar to little Cayou, the Carlisle warrior, and on the massed tackle plays he was given the ball time after time. When tackled he squirmed along the ground like a snake, while in defensive work he broke the interference up well and brought down his man. Shanahan and Linehan, who attended to the end plays, were the life of the Holy Cross eleven, and queered trick plays several times.

The goal which Linehan kicked in the last half brought the spectators to their feet. It was probably the most difficult goal ever accomplished on a grid-

tackle for a slight gain, which was followed by White's plunge for two yards more. The ball was given to Holy Cross at this point on downs, and Kenney, aided by good interference, got 10 yards around Crocker. On the next play Holy Cross was forced to kick. Crocker blocked it, and Boston college had the ball once more. It changed hands again in a few moments, but Holy Cross was unable to do much against the Boston line, and lost the ball on downs.

Vahey decided to give Landrigan opportunity to run, and the snap tackle dove into the line on a formation play, "tackles back," for three yards. The next move was a single criss-cross. The ball was forced back, and White ran to the right. As he was being tackled by Sockalexis he passed the ball to Crocker, who went in the opposite direction. The move was done so quickly that Holy Cross did not see Crocker until he had cleared the line. Then began the race for the goal, the Boston runner having a slight lead. He ran like a deer, but was finally forced outside seven yards from the goal line.

McGrath and White made the necessary five yards, and Boston had the ball on the two-yard line. Another tackle play was made, and Landrigan fell over the line for the first touchdown, 10 minutes after play had begun. Lyons failed to kick the goal.

Holy Cross opened the second half imitating the Boston trick of kicking the ball out of bounds, and on the second try Kenney kicked low. Prendergast stopped it from going outside, but a Worcester man fell on it for a gain of 10 yards. Then the trick plays of Holy Cross were brought out, and by banging away at the tackles and guards the visitors managed to reach the five-yard line. Boston made a magnificent stand but it was no use, and Kelley made the touchdown by his plunge through the line between Long and Prendergast. The goal was kicked by Linehan, and Holy Cross got the lead, 6—4.

The ball changed hands several times after Boston college kicked off, and finally the game ended, as described above, when McGrath attempted to skirt the right end. The summary:

BOSTON COLLEGE	HOLY CROSS
Lyons l e	r e Line
Landrigan l t	r t K
Murphy l g	r g O'
Capt Welsh c	c Campl
Prendergast r g	l g Capt
Long r t	l t Do
Nugent r t	
Crocker r e	l e Shana
Vahey q b	q b Sm
White b b	b b Ke
Brick h b	h b Sockal
Grainger h b	
McGrath f b	f b Hick

Score, Boston college 8, Holy Cross 6. Touchdowns, Landrigan, White, Kelly. from touchdown, Linehan. Umpire, Dadm of W. A. C. Referee, Clarkson of Boston verslty. Linesmen, Drum and ——. Time halves.

1

1887—*With the Indian wars winding to a close, the Northern Pacific Railroad Company invites Sioux Chief Sitting Bull to Bismarck, North Dakota, to be the guest speaker at a celebration of the opening of their transcontinental route. In front of an audience of dignitaries, politicians, and important businessmen, Sitting Bull says: "I hate all white people. You are thieves and liars. You have taken away our lands and made us outcasts." The young army officer translating the chief's words is momentarily flustered but quickly recovers his composure and tells the audience that the chief thanks them and wishes only peace and prosperity between whites and Indians. The crowd gives the chief a standing ovation. Railroad officials are so impressed with Sitting Bull's performance that they ask him to speak at a ceremony to be held a few weeks later in St. Paul, Minnesota. That same year, the U.S. Congress passes the General Allotment (Dawes) Act that would, over time, facilitate the transfer of some sixty-three million acres of Indian land into white hands.*

* * * *

AT ABOUT THE SAME TIME but far from the Indian wars, a young Indian stood in a clearing on the bank of a small island.

Dressed in white man's hand-me-down pants and an old shirt, his skin was bronze and his raven hair long and gleaming. The river, deep and wide, slowly slid by like an old mill hand walking home from a day's work. On the far bank, college boys wearing white sweaters and rosy cheeks played baseball. It was the first time the young Indian saw the white man's game, though ancient members of his tribe played a variation of baseball that dated Alexander Joy Cartwright's version by at least a century or two. The story goes that one day the young Indian paddled his canoe across the Penobscot River and asked if he could shag balls in the outfield during batting practice. Skeptical at first, the players eventually gave in to the Indian's request, then watched slack jawed as the lithe youngster darted around the outfield catching, with his bare hands, every drive hit. But what really astounded the collegians was the boy's throwing arm. Years later, when he became the talk of the National League, there was a story of the young Indian throwing a ball across the river from Old Town, Maine, to Indian Island—more than six hundred feet.

Louis Francis Sockalexis knew nothing of Sitting Bull, the Apache, or Joseph, the famous warrior chief of the Nez Perce, unless he read of them in dime novels. He was a Penobscot. And his tribe had first fought white Europeans two hundred years before the Indian wars. In the 1670s, King Philip of England placed a bounty of five pounds on the scalp of Maine Indians. By 1703 that bounty was forty pounds; by 1744 the payout for the scalp of a male member of the tribes above twelve years of age was fixed at one hundred pounds, and fifty pounds for women and children. Captured tribesmen were sold as slaves. Not only did the English attack Indian villages, killing every man, woman, and child they found, but they burned the settlements to the ground. One of these attacks occurred on Indian Island.

Legend says that tribal shamans foresaw the British crossing of the Penobscot. The night before the attack, elders gathered their families and silently stole away across the moonlit water to the safety of the Maine forest. From there they watched as the English army crossed the Penobscot River at Old Town and burned their ghost village to the ground.

History says the Penobscot rarely ran. When the bloody French and Indian wars prompted many of Maine's Indian tribes to flee to Canada, the Penobscot held fast to Indian Island and their hunting territory along the Penobscot River. Throughout their history, the tribe fiercely defended their land. They mutilated captured warriors—cut off their ears, nose, or hands—and sent them back as a warning to other tribes who dared oppose them. In the 1660s, the tribe fought savage territorial battles with the Mohawks. Vastly outnumbered, the Penobscot suffered greatly. The tragic experience of the Mohawk war prompted the tribe to settle on Indian Island. There they built a fort. Surrounded by the natural mote of the Penobscot River, they successfully turned back attacks by other tribes, including the rapacious Iroquois, who had defeated tribes from the St. Lawrence River to the Mississippi.

For the young Sockalexis, growing up on the reservation was a time of simple and unbridled joy. His father, Francis, was a river guide and an influential elder of the Bear clan. The tribe then was divided into family-controlled hunting stakes, and the Bear clan was the largest. Though little is known of the elder Sockalexis, it seems he nurtured his son's athletic ability. It was said that the father was once the fastest in the tribe, until his son's legs grew strong enough to best him.

Though it is known that Sockalexis played high school baseball and other sports for the Jesuits at St. Ann's Convent School in Old Town, there is then a gap of some years in the recorded history of his baseball career. He surfaces again in an organized league in Van Buren, Maine. There, an athletic director from nearby Houlton offered the young Indian a scholarship to the Ricker Classical Institute, a kind of prep school. For Ricker, Sockalexis both played outfield and pitched. As a pitcher he threw the ball so hard that he once broke the fingers of his catcher's hand. At the same time, he played for the Houlton town team, a member of a local amateur circuit called the Maine–New Brunswick League. That team went 26–2 that season and won the title. After the season, the Houlton team played an exhibition against a collection of college all-stars. It was perhaps then that the legend began to form.

The collegiate pitcher intentionally walked Sockalexis his first three at bats. In the ninth inning the game was tied, 0–0. When the Indian came up in the final frame, he again was issued a base on balls. But this time he took matters into his own hands. He stole second and third and then, crashing into the catcher and knocking the ball free, home. Houlton won the game 1–0. Several news accounts from the time report instances of Sockalexis showing off his prodigious throwing arm. In one, on a dollar bet, he threw a ball over the tower of Hiram Ricker's hotel in Poland Springs, Maine. The tower was 408 feet high. Another tells of his showing off at exhibitions at the Bangor fair, throwing a baseball over the length of the grandstand. Some of the accounts are a bit hard to believe, like the one of him throwing the ball across the Penobscot River. There isn't a major league player today who can throw a ball close to that distance. There was even a story of the Indian skipping a silver dollar over the river.

As early as the 1500s, European fishing boats ventured to the rocky coast of Maine. From these maiden voyages was born a rumor that circulated throughout France that a great and powerful kingdom called Norumbega lay in the valley of the Penobscot—a kingdom filled with riches beyond comprehension. Alas, Frenchmen, like the Spanish conquistadores who searched for the golden cities in America's Southwest, never found the fabled Norumbega. They did, however, find riches. In the early 1600s, after Samuel de Champlain's explorations, the French set up permanent trading posts that would alter forever the future of Maine's Indian tribes. The coastal Indians traded lumber (destined for European ship masts), fish, and most prominently fur for dried foods and metal tools. The Europeans also brought diseases that would decimate the Indian population of Maine. Throughout the1600s and beyond, several epidemics of plague, smallpox, cholera, and other transmittable diseases killed between 90 and 95 percent of the Maine tribes.

French Jesuits first came to Maine with de Champlain in 1604 and would exert enormous influence on the Penobscot and other Maine tribes. In the 1600s, Jesuits sought to isolate and protect Maine's Indians from the evils of European business dealings. At first this aroused the ire of the French government, who saw it as a threat to their lucrative fur concerns. But when the flow of pelts overwhelmed the European market, the government shifted its stance and allowed the Jesuits unhindered access to the tribes. Dating almost from first contact, Jesuits in Maine began a series of correspondences with Society of Jesus leaders in Rome and Paris. *The Relations* was the first detailed body of work to describe life among the inhabitants of the New World. They were also, perhaps, the beginnings of stereotypes that would last for centuries. In 1611, a Jesuit missionary named Pierre Baird wrote this to his superiors in Paris:

> The Nation is savage, wandering and full of bad habits; the people few and isolated. They are, I say, savage, haunting the woods, ignorant, lawless and rude. They are wanderers, with nothing to attach them to place, neither homes nor relationships, neither possessions nor love of country, as a people they had bad habits, are extremely lazy gluttonous, profane, treacherous, cruel in their revenge and given to all kinds of lewdness, men and women alike.

Eventually most Penobscots were converted to Catholicism. By 1703, French Jesuits had taken over the Castine Mission in Old

Town and immediately began to spread the faith. The Jesuits immersed themselves in Penobscot society. They learned the language and customs of the tribe. A Jesuit by the name of Sebastion Rale prepared the first dictionary of the Abenaki language, which included eight different words for moose. But Rale's intimate relationship with Maine's tribes would cost him dearly. He was killed by British troops at his mission in Norridgewock, Maine, in 1724.

In 1894, while playing summer ball for a team in Poland Springs, Sockalexis met Michael "Doc" Powers, the captain of the Holy Cross baseball team, and his life would change forever. By the 1890s baseball had become a phenomenon on college campuses throughout the northeast. In 1891 the Holy Cross baseball team played fourteen games, mostly against the Ivy League teams of Brown, Harvard, and Yale. By 1894 the schedule was expanded to twenty-four. Victories on the field were wildly celebrated with bonfires, parades, fireworks, and of course drinking beer. The school was so caught up in baseball fever that professors used memorable plays as metaphors in lectures on Cicero. Home games regularly attracted crowds of four thousand and more. In 1893, to accommodate the bulging attendance, Holy Cross built a stadiumlike field on a lower terrace of the hilly campus.

At Doc Powers's urging, Sockalexis enrolled in Holy Cross in the fall of 1894. His academics were actually conducted at Holy Cross prep. In those days, before SATs and high school requirements, most major universities had preparatory schools on campus to ensure a high level of academic standards. A local newspaper, the *Worcester Post*, trumpeted his arrival:

> A new ball player will soon be added to the list of strong amateur players already at Holy Cross. He is Louis Sockalexis, of Old Town, Maine. He is a star all-around player who will make an excellent man for the outfield or the bases. For the past two years he had played on the Poland Spring [*sic*] team with Captain Powers of the Holy Cross nine. Last season he received an offer from the New England League, but he preferred to remain in the ranks of the amateurs and continue his studies. . . . It begins to look like '95 will be a banner athletic year at Holy Cross.

The Worcester paper was prophetic. "Sox" or "Sock," as he was first called while playing in Poland Springs, quickly attained stardom at Holy Cross. And, like most of his career, the line between fact and myth was blurred. What is documented during his two years at Holy Cross is that Sockalexis batted .436 and .444 respectively. He hit from the left side of the plate but threw with his right hand. Led by the Indian, the 1895 team compiled a record of 17–5–2. In his first game in Crusader purple, Sockalexis had three triples.

The baseball program's success emboldened the college spirit on the Holy Cross campus. After a road win against league powerhouse Brown in 1895, half the boarding student body went AWOL from school grounds—strictly forbidden then—to meet the team at Worcester's train depot. The game record shows that Sockalexis had four hits that day, including a home run. He also stole six bases—four for the Brown team. A Brown player had injured his ankle, and under the rules of the day the Brown captain selected Sockalexis from the opposing bench to run for him. Sock went on to steal four bases for Brown and two for his own team. Though his base running was documented, the home run he hit that day resides in lore. The ball allegedly traveled more than five hundred feet and broke a window of the university's chapel some distance beyond the outfield fence.

Later that season, in a game against Harvard held at Holy Cross, a ball was hit over Sock's head in center field. According to a Worcester newspaper account, the ball rolled out of the field of play—there was no outfield fence—and onto a neighboring tennis court. "He was after the ball in a flash," the newspaper said, "and made a lightening [sic] throw, landing the ball into the pitcher's box and reducing a home run to a three-base hit." Two Harvard professors in attendance that day calculated the throw at 414 feet.

The legend of Sockalexis grew as the season continued, with newspapers perpetuating and inflating the tale. One story told of a home run that broke a fourth-story dormitory window; another said that Sockalexis had swum across the Blackstone River, which bordered the Holy Cross field, to catch a fly ball on the far bank. Though statistics bear out that exaggeration was unnecessary, you can't really blame the writers of the day. To them, Sockalexis was a mysterious character, almost mythical. He was tall, handsome, and solidly built—the Abenaki Adonis and Deerfoot of the Diamond they called him. But the mystery, as most are, was rooted in ignorance and stereotype. The truth was, he was very much like any other eastern college boy of that era.

There is a picture of Sockalexis from his days at Holy Cross. His hair is fashionably cut, he wears a college sweater over his shoulders, and he sports a small, mischievous college-boy grin. Throughout his baseball life, and for nearly a hundred years after, news writers and biographers cared more about the myth and less about the man. But perhaps the real reason behind the mythmaking was the Indian's timing.

When the English landed at Plymouth Rock, a power struggle over land and commerce in America developed between the French and the British. The Penobscot, along with other Abenaki tribes from what is now Maine, formed a loose confederation with the French against the English. An Abenaki narrative of the day explains why the once-warring tribes joined together:

> Long ago, the Indians were always fighting against each other. They struck one another bloodily. There were many men, women and children who alike were tormented by these constant battles. . . . It seemed as if all were tired of how they had lived wrongly. The great chiefs said to the others, "Looking back from here the way we have come, we see that we have left bloody tracks. We see may wrongs. And as for these bloody hatchets, and bows, arrows, they must be buried forever." Then they all set about deciding to join with one another in a confederacy.

The Penobscot took the side of the colonists during the Revolution. Though the Daughters of the American Revolution would, after the war, raise a monument honoring the brave Abenaki who fought and died alongside the colonial troops, the truth was that the Maine Indians gave only tepid support to the Revolutionists. As much as they hated the English, the Penobscots didn't need shamans to foresee the colonists stealing their land. By 1796, the Penobscot had ceded all but Indian Island and several other islands in the Penobscot River to Massachusetts, whose territory then encompassed most of what is now Maine. Massachusetts became the governing body that oversaw the Penobscot tribe, as the federal government viewed them as "domesticated Indians." In 1820, Maine was granted statehood, and the Penobscot became its wards. It was then that Indian Island officially became a reservation.

The society of the Penobscot tribe strengthened as their land shrunk. In late summer, bonfires blazed in celebration of the season's change. Men wagered on games of chance. Dice were made from antlers. Women worked together weaving baskets, which were sold to white visitors. The Maine Indian took advantage of stereotypes. By the late 1800s, tribe members formed traveling medicine shows, dressing like Apache braves to add drama to their appearance. Tonics that "thickened the blood" were sold for a dollar. Still, especially among the Penobscot, there was a fierce pride. Elders commanded the utmost respect. Tribal lore was handed down to the younger generations. Stories of the great battles of the Penobscot past were kept alive with these remembrances.

The Penobscot River was the sustenance of life for the Indians who lived in its valley. In the fragrant spring and lush, warm summer, Penobscots hunted the dense forest along the banks. Perch, bass, and eels were caught and smoked to provide food for the long Maine winters. For the Penobscot, the river and its environs was a mythical place. The name Penobscot means "rocky place," and the tribe believed that among these rocks lived *wannagames'nak*, mischievous leprechaun-like creatures who would steal food and frighten women. The women of the Penobscot tribe dug ginseng root, which they believed helped fertility. Men of the tribe were deft at navigating the river and fishing from canoes made of moose skin. Lumber companies noticed this talent. By the 1800s the river was a conduit on which logs were driven to mills downstream. Wood then played the same role that fossil fuel does today, and the river was black with lumber oil. Penobscots were hired to drive the logs in large canoes called bateaux. Stories of these river drivers proliferate in publications of the time.

In 1853 writer Henry David Thoreau visited the Maine woods. He was shown the river and its environs by Penobscot River guides like Joseph Aitteon, who attained legendary status through Thoreau's stories. Here's Thoreau's description from *Walden* of meeting Joe Aitteon, in the Chesuncook essay in "The Maine Woods":

I was here first introduced to Joe. He had ridden all the way on the outside of the stage, the day before, in the rain, giving way to ladies, and was well wetted. As it still rained, he asked if we were going to "put it through." He was a good-looking Indian, twenty-four years old, apparently of unmixed blood, short and stout, with a broad face and reddish complexion, and eyes, methinks, narrower and more turned-up at the outer corners than ours, answering to the description of his race. Beside his under-clothing, he wore a red-flannel shirt, woolen pants, and a black Kossuth hat, the ordinary dress of the lumberman, and, to a considerable extent, of the Penobscot Indian.

Though logging brought great wealth to company owners, poverty on the reservation was acute. Still, the Penobscot children's laughter could be heard from across the river. Games of competition were commonplace. One game's literal translation was Throw the Ball. The rules were simple: Whoever could throw the ball farthest won. The tribe's form of baseball was played on a field with four posts at the corners, complete with a pitcher, catcher, and batter. The ball was softball size or larger, pliable, and covered with animal skin. The bat was a thick, honed branch. The batter would hit the pitch and then run around the posts. When the pitcher was able to knock the ball down or catch it on a fly four times, the batter was out.

Just one year before Sockalexis arrived at Holy Cross, a little-known history professor named Frederick Jackson Turner delivered at the Chicago World's Fair what would become the most famous academic paper in America's history. It was Turner's assertion that America's democracy depended on a frontier: "The paths of pioneers have widened into broad highways. The forest clearing has expanded into affluent commonwealths. Let us see to it that the ideals of the pioneer in his log cabin shall enlarge into the spiritual life of a democracy where civil power shall dominate and utilize individual achievement for the common good."

Three years before Turner delivered his thesis, the 1890 census had pronounced the frontier dead. Turner wondered what was to become of us. In the late 1800s the industrialization and swelling of cities left little room for the frontier spirit. At the same time, a game called baseball evolved and captured the imagination of America. The game became a frontier of sorts for industrialized cities in America's Northeast. Baseball was the vast flowing fields of wheat of which Thomas Jefferson had dreamt. Unlike his intellectual adversary, Alexander Hamilton, who foresaw that America's power lay in banking and industry, Jefferson longed for a country carpeted with a golden harvest. In some ways, baseball linked these two ideals. In a giant industrialized metropolis, a shimmering diamond of green grass could exist and thrive.

Though Turner's model conveniently left out what has been termed the American Holocaust—at first contact with whites the Native population of what is now America was estimated at ten million; it had dropped to fewer than a quarter million at the taking of the 1890 census—the image of the Indian was, in the American psyche, the penultimate symbol of the frontier. As Sockalexis biographer Luke Salisbury once wrote: "One could argue that the national game changed from killing Indians to baseball sometime after 1876." So here was Sockalexis, seemingly walking out of the old frontier and into the new one—baseball. At the same time, Sockalexis walked into the dreams of every sportswriter who had the good fortune to watch him play.

One story that elevated myth into the theater of the absurd has been retold over the years many times. It goes like this: When the young Sockalexis first decided to attend Holy Cross, his father paddled a canoe down the Penobscot River, along the eastern coastline, and up the Potomac to Washington, D.C. There he asked the Great White Father, President Cleveland, to make his son a chief so he wouldn't play the white man's game. According to the story in the *Sporting News*, the president granted the elder Sockalexis's request, but by the time he had paddled all the way back to the reservation his son had already left for school.

Though college historians place athletic scholarships to baseball players as far back as the 1870s, Holy Cross did not indulge in the practice until the 1890s. Even then, only one full scholarship was awarded. Still, the school realized that intercollegiate sports were quickly rivaling academic prowess in enrollment drawing power. Simply put, college sports, and baseball in particular, was great advertisement for the school. Though it's not known how much of a scholarship Sockalexis was offered, considering the poverty on Indian Island, the school's financial help had to be considerable. Perhaps it is only coincidental that Holy Cross began to charge admission to baseball games—fifteen cents for students, a quarter for general admission—around the time Sockalexis roamed center field for them. One thing is certain, however: For the rest of Sock's baseball life, management and ownership measured his worth in gate receipts.

The school also took advantage of baseball's popularity by scheduling games outside the college ranks. In 1895, Holy Cross played the vaunted Cuban Giants. Originally a team made up of black porters to entertain guests at a posh Long Island hotel, the Giants had become a traveling sensation. There were no Cubans on the team, but the name was affixed to the club as a way to side-step the stigma then surrounding black ballplayers. The Cuban Giants were led by Ulysses F. "Frank" Grant, one of the premier black players of the nineteenth century. Though the contest was game, the Holy Cross nine lost to the Giants, 6–5.

College campuses were not the only place with baseball fever. The whole of New England burned hot with it. There were scores of baseball leagues, from the more haphazardly formed county variety to the semiprofessional. In the summer of 1895, Powers signed with the Warren Spiders of the Knox County League in northern Maine. On the strength of his 1895 season at Holy Cross, Sockalexis was already well known in the area, and Powers easily convinced Spiders' manager Ed Teague to also sign the Indian. On June 25, 1895, the *Warren Newsletter* announced Sock's arrival. "He is an awful slugger," the article stated, "a sure catch, is as fleet as a deer, and can throw as straight and as far as a new fashioned rifle."

Though it's not known what salary Sockalexis signed for, the going rate for star players in that league was $45 dollars a week, plus room and board—a handsome deal for any working man at that time, let alone a college boy. But Sock's salary might have been even greater. "It is costing the Warren Baseball Association $125 a week for players now," reported the *Newsletter*. Doc Powers might have been the force behind the inflated salaries in that league. In 1890 one of the Knox County team's managers was Burt L. Standish, a well-known dime novelist in his real life. A writer of Dickensian prolificity, Standish wrote under the pen name Gilbert Patten. According to a biography of Patten, Powers once held the league owners hostage by offering his services as a player "at a prohibitive cost." The Knox County team owners told Powers to "roll his hoop." But Powers got his revenge—and his money—by forming his own team made up of fellow Holy Cross players.

(According to some historians, Sockalexis was the inspiration for Standish/Patten's wildly popular dime novel character Frank Merriwell. This seems unlikely, as Merriwell was not Native American; his father was a wealthy mine owner who left his family after becoming a degenerate gambler. Though the Merriwell character was a successful and popular college baseball star in the Northeast, he attended Yale, not Holy Cross, and graduated with "the highest honors." There is a chance a minor character in the Merriwell saga, which spawned 280 novels between 1896 and 1916, was based on Sockalexis. But more than likely, Sockalexis was part of the amalgam that was Frank Merriwell. An Indian ballplayer might have been fodder for mythical tales in newspaper stories but not for a dime novel character that reached the homes of hundreds of thousands of white American boys. America was not ready for a wholesome Indian hero. Perhaps Sockalexis's contribution to the character was Merriwell's flare for dramatics on the baseball diamond, a trait the author undoubtedly admired about the Indian.)

Regardless of his salary, with the Indian's arrival teams in the Knox County League had little trouble in meeting payroll thanks to an increase in attendance. Sock was a gate attraction, and big news. "Sockalexis is catching on in great shape in Warren, equal to President Cleveland during his first term. There is already a cat named for him—we mean Sock, not Cleveland," said the *Warren Newsletter.* In one game's box score, Sock was five for seven at the plate, and the game's summary described one of his throws from center field as "phenomenal," nailing a runner who tagged from third at home plate for a double play.

Back at Holy Cross the Indian excelled in sports other than baseball. He was clocked at a ten-second-flat hundred-yard dash, then the fastest time in the country. He also competed in the four-man relay on the track team. At first his inexperience showed itself in his unwieldy style. Jostling for position, he once knocked a teammate off the track. A bit overanxious, he had a penchant for stumbling at the start. But more often than not his raw speed made up for any technical shortcomings. In a much-anticipated match against Yale, Sock ran the third leg of a relay. His teammate fell on the second leg and by the time he recovered and passed the baton to Sockalexis, Yale had a seemingly insurmountable twenty-five-yard lead. On the first lap of his leg Sock made up little ground.

But as they turned for the second lap, he turned on the speed. When he passed the baton to the team anchor, he had pulled almost even, and Holy Cross won the relay.

Sockalexis was also a star for the Holy Cross football team and was involved in one of the most controversial games that program has ever played—a match against rival Boston College on November 14, 1896. Late in the game, Holy Cross led 6–4—touchdowns were then counted as four points—mostly on the strength of Sockalexis's running. With four minutes remaining in the game, Boston College drove the ball deep into the Holy Cross end of the field. A Boston College runner named McGrath headed around end and for a moment looked to be in the clear. But Sockalexis broke through the line and dumped McGrath for a loss of three yards. The tackle, a particularly hard one, drew the ire of the hometown Boston College fans. Students streamed from the grandstand and onto the field and attacked the Holy Cross team. According to the *Worcester Telegraph*, the Boston College faithful outnumbered the Holy Cross men ten to one. "For more than five minutes the air was filled with flying canes, fists and hats. The mob had attacked the handful of Holy Cross men and was tossing and knocking them around in a most brutal manner," the paper reported. Local police arrived and brought a semblance of order.

In the confusion a Boston College player picked up the ball and ran it across the Holy Cross goal line. At first the officials disallowed the play and, having lost control, signaled the game's end. The Holy Cross coach pulled his team from the field and headed for the safety of the locker room. But bending to the hometown pressure, the refs again conferred. With the Holy Cross team already in the locker room, the referees allowed the late touchdown, deciding that Holy Cross had no right to leave the field. The following day the *Boston Globe* heralded an 8–6 Boston College victory, but the *Boston Journal*, whose sportswriter must have left the game a bit early, wrote of the home team suffering a crushing 6–4 defeat. Father James Gardiner, a member of the Holy Cross faculty, penned the sentiment of that school: "In consequence of Boston College uniform dishonest & ungentlemanly conduct—Holy Cross will not, either in Foot or Base, Ball again contend with Boston College." To this day, Boston College remains Holy Cross's most hated rival.

By 1896 the *Sporting News*, then a new national weekly, ranked the Holy Cross baseball team as one of the best college teams ever assembled. Five players from the 1895 edition would go on to the major leagues. The school luxuriated in its fame. Where once they traded barbs with schools like Boston College, now they didn't even bother. With two more years of the Indian in center field, the future of the national spotlight never looked so bright. But Sockalexis and Powers would not play the 1897 season for Holy Cross. And the two star players' departure from the college was filled with acrimony.

On December 17, the *Worcester Daily Spy* wrote: "The students of Holy Cross College, especially those who are interested in the welfare of the base ball team, were given a very disagreeable surprise Wednesday night when it was announced that Captain Michael R. Powers, the crack catcher of the nine, was to sever his connection with the college to enter the University of Notre Dame at South Bend, Indiana." The following day that same publication stated: "Following close upon the heels of the going away from Holy Cross College of Michael Powers . . . comes the news that Louis F. Sockalexis, the full-blooded Indian athlete, who has done much good work at Holy Cross in the past two years, has also left the college, with the same destination in view as Powers. The faculty are not much pleased with the manner in which Sockalexis took his leave." The school newspaper did say that from the beginning of his tenure at Holy Cross, Sockalexis "was popular with the faculty and students, as well as all who took interest in the athletics of the college."

According to a written account by the ministers of Holy Cross, the University of Notre Dame offered money to lure Powers to South Bend. To assume that Notre Dame was using Powers as a way to also acquire Sockalexis would be pure speculation. Still, it's a good guess. Though Powers was a collegiate star in his own right, he paled next to the publicity nova surrounding Sockalexis. One Holy Cross father called the Notre Dame offer "a bribe" and accused Powers of not having the spirit to refuse. There were no regulations, no NCAA to oversee scholarships and other incentives offered to student athletes. The Indian's stay at South Bend, however, would be brief. And by all accounts his hasty departure would both make him the talk of the nation and begin his downfall.

HERE IT IS AGAIN.

The Old, Old Story, With a Few Slight Variations.

Louisville Now Starts the Rumor.

The Falls City a Little Late, but It Finally Falls in Line—The Indians Start on the Practice Trip — Corbett and Fitzsimmons Will Now Begin Over Again—Bicycling News and Other Sporting.

The prophecy was made in this paper yesterday that the Cleveland transfer story would break out again pretty soon, for two reasons: First, President Robison left the city, and second, the story has not been told for over a week, and is therefore due. It has arrived on time, but on account of the second reason. Just wait until it becomes noised about the country that Mr. Robison has gone to meet John T. Brush of Cincinnati, and then look out! In the meantime, the story has been dug up through less suspicious circumstances. A dispatch from Louisville gives the following startling information: Notwithstanding all the denials and contradictions of stories

SOCKALEXIS.

in regard to the transfer of the Clevelands or change in the circuit of the big league, here is no question but that an important move will be made early in May, if Sunday ball is interfered with in Cleveland

ing arms in this city, with Zimmer as a receiver, and Harry Blake will cultivate his batting eye on their curves.

Australians Arrive.

SAN FRANCISCO, April 9.—The Australian baseball players, who are starting out on a tour of the world, have arrived in this city on the steamer Monowai. They will spend a few days in sight seeing before practicing for their opening game, which will be with the Olympics a week from Sunday at Central park.

The nervy athletes who have come thousands of miles to ascertain how the best baseball players of Australia compare with those in this country, and to learn points if deficient, are thirteen in number. The team has several substitutes, so they may play cricket as well as baseball. The players are: Frank Laver, captain, pitcher and first base; Charles Kemp, a "south paw" twirler; James McKay, pitcher and catcher; R. E. Ewers, pitcher and catcher; Sydney Smith, first base and change catcher; Walter Ingleton, second base; Peter A. McAllister, third base; Harry Irwin, short stop; Alfred S. Carter, left fielder; A. E. Wiseman, center fielder; Harry Stuckey, right fielder; J. L. Wallace, catcher; Charles Over, all-around man. R. E. Ewers is the champion all-around athlete of Australia.

Bierbauer Retires.

ERIE, Pa., April 9.—Louis Bierbauer, one of the greatest second basemen in the country, has gone into business here and announces his retirement from the diamond. There are still many years of baseball in Bierbauer, but he does not like the terms of his transfer to St. Louis by the Pittsburg club. The price paid by St. Louis for Bierbauer's services is reported at $1,500, but whether the Pittsburg club can claim the money under the circumstances is doubtful. Von Der Ahe will certainly demand the goods before paying over the sum; although it is stated that Bierbauer had signed a St. Louis contract.

Bierbauer's injured ankle, which is said to have been responsible for his transfer, is entirely well, but Louis has a notion that he can make more money in business than on the diamond.

PUGILISM.

Mrs. Fitz is Angry.

Mrs. Bob Fitzsimmons, who is the only one of the whole Carson City aggregation who is at all backward about rushing into print, was interviewed by a Salt Lake City newspaper man who says:

Mrs. Robert Fitzsimmons is a reticent body when a newspaper man asks her to tell about the fight at Carson. She refuses at those times to talk. But when a woman worms herself into her confidence and asks a lot of questions, Mrs. Fitz will become even voluble in her conversation.

"Why did I go to the fight?" she asked, answering one question by putting another. "Well, because I was interested in my husband's success. There has been a great deal told about Bob being all bloody and all that. To be sure he was. His nose bled, but I saw it worse one time when he bumped against a door in the night.

"I knew Mr. Fitzsimmons would beat him just as soon as they entered the ring. He looked over at me and winked, as much as to say, 'I will beat him before he knows it.' Corbett guyed me a little by looking at me and smiling in such

2

1897—In early March, Ohio's William McKinley is escorted by the 1st Cleveland Cavalry to Washington, D.C., to be sworn in as the twenty-fifth president of the United States. With the cooperation of Thomas A. Edison, Cleveland's own William C. Baker develops an automobile run on electricity, his streamlined "Torpedo" car, which makes news worldwide. On March 21 the official account of Cleveland's one hundredth birthday is published; the previous year's centennial celebration had included ten days of parades, speeches, and gatherings. In April, President McKinley presides over the dedication of Grant's Tomb in New York. One of the guests of honor at the ceremony is Chief Joseph, the legendary Nez Perce warrior, who meets with his once-hated adversary, General Howard, at New York's Astor House.

* * * *

THE 1800S IN AMERICA was a time when a few ruthless individuals gained most of the country's wealth. Banker J. P. Morgan once refused a loan to the U.S. government because, he said, it lacked collateral. Cleveland's John D. Rockefeller began his business career as an accountant, heading a firm that investigated the potential of oil investments. He told his own employees there was no future in oil, then wholeheartedly invested in the natural resource himself. Owners of the teams in baseball's National League, then, were aptly named magnates. Rich and dictatorial, these men mirrored the industrial and banking titans of the time. Indeed, geographically the game was confined mostly to the burgeoning industrial centers of the Northeast.

Organized baseball originated as a gentlemen's game played by "sporting" amateurs of strictly upper-class stripe. The New York Knickerbockers was one such team—they played the game dressed in vests and ties. But as the popularity of the sport brought spectators to matches, more emphasis was placed on ability. This dynamic opened the game to the lower-economic class of players who were admitted into the exclusive club on the basis of talent.

As the game evolved in skill, even more fans came to watch. Eventually business-minded people saw an opportunity for financial gain. Leagues were organized, ballparks were fitted with bleachers, and of course fees for admission were established. By the 1890s there were twelve National League clubs, each with a roster of (only) fifteen players. Besides inherent racism, the scarcity of jobs led to the league's policy of exclusion. The talent of Negro ballplayers of the time, and later the Negro leagues, was an overwhelming threat to the white players.

And so it was that while Sockalexis was playing ball for Holy Cross, baseball in Cleveland had grown from a curiosity and gentlemen's game to nearly an obsession. It had surely become a business. The team belonged to one Frank De Hass Robison. A prototype of the magnate owners of the day, Robison was the model of the fat-cat owners who loomed in baseball's future. He acquired his wealth with the help of a fortuitous marriage. Sarah C. Hathaway was the daughter of Philadelphia's Charles Hathaway, a builder of street railcars and tracks. Hathaway's new son-in-law did not idle in his newfound wealth but proved to have a head for business. The reach of the Hathaway and Robison Company, formed in 1877, soon stretched from New Orleans to Fargo, from Maine to California. Robison, always with an eye on virgin markets, saw great potential in the city of Cleveland, which had swelled from a paltry population of seventeen thousand in 1850 to more than a quarter million people by 1880. Splitting from his father-in-law in this venture, Robison personally oversaw the construction of cable lines in Cleveland. The lines were built on Superior, St. Clair, and Payne Avenues. It was the Payne Avenue line that would lead to Robison's baseball life.

In 1886, James Williams, the manager of the Columbus, Ohio, team in the American Association of baseball clubs, met Robison in the lobby of the Euclid Hotel and suggested that a lot just off the Payne Avenue line at 39th Street would be the perfect spot for a professional ballpark. Robison was never one to miss out on a good idea. Though Cleveland was already rich in baseball history—in 1869 the city fielded the Red Stockings, its first semiprofessional team—it had been without a professional franchise since 1885. After a dismal showing that season and star player defections to St. Louis, the Cleveland team had folded.

Soon after his meeting with Williams, Robison vowed to bring a professional team back to Cleveland, "if I have to buy a team myself, sell the tickets, and haul it around in my own streetcars," he once said. Undoubtedly it was the hauling around in his streetcars part of his statement that was the most important. As he sat on the leather wing chair in the restaurant in the big hotel, his business mind whirled with the vision of the growing horde of Cleveland's baseball cranks, as fans were called back then, paying him the penny cable car fare, then reaching back into their patched trousers to fork up another fifty cents for entrance into his park.

Robison named George W. Howe, a prominent local citizen and nephew of sewing machine inventor Elias Howe, as the treasurer of his baseball venture. In December of 1886, Howe attended a meeting of the American Association. There the directors of the league dropped the financially struggling Pittsburgh franchise and voted Cleveland in. The team was called the Forest Citys, resurrecting the name of the old team. Forest City was Cleveland's nickname. It is said that former mayor William Case was responsible for the moniker because of his crusade to plant fruit and shade trees throughout the city. Though the team finished dead last that 1887 season, the Forest Citys were a hit with a growing working class in Cleveland.

During the summer of 1888, Robison lobbied hard for acceptance in the more stable and lucrative National League. His efforts were rewarded at the close of that season when the league dropped the Detroit team. Though Robison was the driving force behind the team, Howe was more involved in day-to-day operations. He outfitted the players in spiffy white and dark blue uniforms and was instrumental in renaming the club. The story goes that while watching the team practice that spring he bemoaned to a local sportswriter the fact that the players' anatomies didn't do justice to their new uniforms. "They look awful," he reportedly said. "All skinny and spindly. They're nothing more than spiders." The name caught on with Cleveland's ink-stained scribes and became the team's official nickname.

The Spiders and their antecedents, the Forest Citys, were somewhat less than a league powerhouse. They finished last in 1888, and after a promising start in 1889 went 7–19 in August and finished in the second division. Still, fans in Cleveland embraced them. Part of the reason was that the team mirrored the city's rough-and-tumble persona. In the midst of that August winning streak the team attacked an umpire after a controversial call that went the opposing team's way. In the stands fans howled their approval. The police arrived and ultimately secured the ump's safety. For the rest of the game police lined the field to keep the simmering crowd from finishing what the Spiders had started.

Under Robison's and Howe's tutelage, the Spiders wouldn't stay mired in the second division for long. A strong lineup, which included future Hall of Famer Oliver Wendell "Patsy" Tebeau and an Ohio farm boy by the name of Denton True "Cy" Young, would make them title contenders well into the 1890s. The beginning of their rise to the top of the league was like a scene out of the movie *The Natural*. During a game on a warm June day in 1890, a fast-moving thunderstorm moved across Lake Erie, draping the field in darkness. Thunder rumbled ominously above. Heeding the warning, the crowd streamed from the grandstand just as lightning pierced the black sky. A bolt struck the stands, and flaming pieces of wood fell to the ground.

The 1891 season saw the opening of the Spiders' new home: League Park. Of course the location, Lexington Avenue and East 66th Street, was just steps away from a Robison streetcar line. For the first game played at the new field, ten thousand paying customers packed the grandstand. A writer from the *Cleveland Plain Dealer* described it like this:

> The grounds at 4 o'clock, viewed from the field, were a sight long to be remembered. The three big stands were black with a mass of dark colored coats and hats. Here and there in the grand stand was a little knot of color, relieving the monotony of it all like a flower bed placed in the center of a well kept lawn. For ten feet in front of the pavilion the people sat and stood on the grass as thickly placed as—well, the proverbial sardines in a box will do for comparison's sake. The crowd drifted into right field, just outside the foul line, and from there all around the field near the fences the folks stood.

A brass band played for hours before the game as the cranks streamed into the park. For the occasion, gentlemen dressed in Sunday best, some with women attired "handsomely" on their arms. Bouquets of flowers were handed to veteran players who blushed and bowed to the faithful. The throng erupted in a roar when Cy Young's pitch split the plate for strike one of the game. The *Plain Dealer* declared: "Baseball is back in Cleveland!"

Throughout the 1891 season, cranks crammed into Robison's streetcars to watch the Spiders play. They weren't disappointed. Cy Young won thirty-six games and lost only ten. Patsy Tebeau was elevated from team captain to player-manager and was an inspiration to his mates as well as the bane of existence to umpires throughout the league. (Tebeau had led the charge in the ump-bashing game of 1889.) In 1892 the National League expanded by four teams. That year the league played a split season, with an end-of-the-year playoff between the season's first-half winner and the second-half champ. Though the Spiders didn't play as well as expected during the first months of the season, they roared through the latter part of the summer, chalking up fifty-three wins against only twenty-three defeats and taking the second-half crown. The Championship Series pitted Cleveland against the hated Boston Beaneaters. Most of the ire of the locals was directed at Mike "King" Kelly, who was without question baseball's first megastar.

In 1887 the Boston Beaneaters had bought Kelly from Chicago for the then unheard-of price of ten thousand dollars. Though there was a two-thousand-dollar cap on players' salaries, the Boston team circumvented the limit by paying Kelly an extra three thousand dollars a year for the right to use his picture in team advertising.

He was also something of a star on the vaudeville stage, where he would recite "Casey at the Bat," usually to a full house.

The overwhelmingly Irish and Irish-American fan base in Boston reveled in Kelly's arrival. In saloons throughout the city a picture of Kelly sliding into second replaced the popular painting of Custer's Last Stand. Beaneaters fans gifted the star with an expensive carriage, drawn by white stallions, which Kelly would ride through the Boston streets on his way to the ballpark. At night he would prowl Boston's saloons and dance halls dressed in the finest suit with an ascot held by a gaudy jewel. "He walked with a cane a'twirling as though he were the entire population," said one Boston newspaperman.

Kelly was, in the vernacular of the day, a lusher. But far from being considered a shortcoming, his prodigious drinking exalted him in the eyes of his following. He was known for wandering to the stands before the start of an inning and imbibing in a glass of "German tea" with the rowdy Boston fans. Once asked if he ever drank while he was playing, Kelly answered, "It depends on the length of the game." The King would often arrive at the games right from a night of carousing—if he showed at all. He was particularly fond of Cleveland's nightlife.

In 1889, with Boston involved in a heated pennant race with the New York Giants, the Beaneaters played a pivotal late-season game in Cleveland. The King arrived at League Field still drunk from the night before. The Boston manager, Jim Hart, wouldn't allow the star to play. Kelly still managed to cause a ruckus while sitting on the bench in street clothing. After a call on a close play at the plate went the Spiders' way, Kelly rushed the umpire and was forcibly removed from the park by police. (Kelly was a no-show for a game against the Spiders earlier that 1891 season. He was found later that day sleeping it off in a boardinghouse with a less than reputable reputation. The slap on the wrist, in the form of a ten-dollar fine, and the accompanying press about the incident only added to his reputation.)

By 1892 Kelly's career had begun to decline badly. He played only the first two games of the Championship Series against Cleveland and went hitless in eight chances at the plate. He did almost manage to pull off one of his old tricks. In the ninth inning of the scoreless first game, Boston teammate Jack Stivetts hit a high pop-up just in front of home plate. Cleveland's catcher, "Chief" Zimmer, settled in to make the catch. From the bench, the King loudly shouted "Virtue!"—the name of the Cleveland first baseman. Thinking a teammate was calling on him to make the play, Virtue slammed into Zimmer. Both players ended up tangled on the ground, but Zimmer somehow was able to make the catch. Patsy Tebeau screamed for Kelly to be thrown out of the game. Cooler heads finally prevailed, and darkness ended the contest in a 0–0 tie. Despite the King's poor performance, Boston went on to win the next five games to capture the best-of-nine series.

The King's rapacious habit ended tragically in early November of 1894. On a ferry to Boston where he was to again recite "Casey at the Bat" at the Palace Theater, he gave his overcoat to a stowaway shivering on the deck. Freezing wind and heavy snow pummeled the boat all the way to Boston Harbor. By the time the King descended the gangplank, he was wet with fever. For several days he lay in a friend's house in various stages of consciousness. Finally he was brought to Boston's Emergency Hospital. While being helped in the door, he slipped to his knees and remarked: "That's my last slide." He died in the hospital bed on the evening of November 8. The following day the headline in the *New York Times* read: "King Kelly Dies of Pneumonia."

The professional baseball player of the late 1800s most likely had a hard-knock life. By then, immigrants and first-generation Americans played the game as well as filled the stands. According to baseball historian Lee Allen, more than 90 percent of the players of that decade traced their ancestry to Ireland, England, and Germany. Drinking and the hard life was a large part of their heritage, and it influenced how they played the game.

The working-class fans of the day identified with the players' dirty fingernails, gnarly hands, and propensity for the drink. Heroes like Boston's King Kelly arose from the grime to be deified. In fact, as long as a player performed, the more human foibles he exhibited the more likely he was to be worshiped. For those unfortunate players who gained adoration from the fans but couldn't hold their drink, time in the spotlight was short, unhappy, and sometimes ended tragically. After he was suspended from the Washington Senators for chronic drinking, star player Ed Delahanty boarded a train in Chicago and headed back east. During the trip he caused a commotion and was put off in Canada. A boarder watchman stopped him as he tried to enter the United States by bridge over the Niagara River. A scuffle ensued and Delahanty fell from the bridge. His body was found some miles downstream, below Niagara Falls.

Some in the National League tried to curtail alcohol abuse. A. G. Spaulding, the owner of the Chicago franchise and later a sporting-goods magnate, offered bonuses to star players who could sustain sobriety. Spaulding was the first to send his team to a warm climate for spring training. But the trip to Hot Springs, Arkansas, had more to do with sobering up the team than sharpening their winter-rusty baseball skills. When a sportswriter asked Spaulding why Hot Springs, the magnate replied: "To boil the alcohol microbes out of them."

Most teams of Kelly's era employed detectives to keep players out of trouble and, hopefully, sober. In 1880 the league banished the Cincinnati team for selling liquor at their ballpark. In 1882 ten players deemed by the National League president William A. Hulbert as "chronic lushers" were banned for life.

Though Cleveland would lose to Boston and King Kelly in 1892, the Spiders had found a home in the Forest City, and in 1895 they again would play for the league championship, now called the Temple Cup. In 1893, William Temple, the president of the Pittsburgh franchise, purposed that a playoff be held for the first- and second-place finishers at season's end. He'd even throw in the cup itself at a cost of about eight hundred dollars. The league knew a good deal when it saw one, and passed the measure. Cleveland earned its second-place finish that year mostly on the strength of the play of their center fielder, Jesse "Crab" Burkett.

In 1891, Robison was able to finagle a deal with the New York Giants to buy Burkett's contract. It was one of the best deals the Spiders would make. In 1892, Burkett's first full year with Cleveland, he hit only .275. But over the next three seasons his average steadily increased; in 1895, he hit .423. And he was more than just a bat. As quick as a jackrabbit, Burkett was the best leadoff man in the league. A terror on the base paths, and with the likes of Tebeau, "Cupid" Childs, and Ed McKean batting behind him, he was almost a cinch to score each time he reached base. As a fielder he was without peer. With Burkett in center, the Spiders almost didn't need a right and left fielder.

Furthermore, Burkett wasn't called "Crab" because of his love of seafood; he fit right in with the Spiders temperament. In one game in Louisville, Burkett led an all-out assault on the opposing team. The donnybrook ended with several Louisville players needing medical attention and the entire Spider team under arrest. Burkett and his teammates spent the night in a Louisville jail. At the arraignment the next morning the judge levied fines of fifty dollars to one hundred dollars—a healthy sum in those days. The old man himself, Robison, ponied up the dough, and undoubtedly, as his team's antics were retold in every sports section across the country, the magnate smiled as he peeled the bills off his roll. Tebeau once proudly proclaimed: "A milk and water, goody-goody player can't ever wear a Cleveland uniform."

With Tebeau as his manager and baseball man, Robison's Spiders were tough and talented where baseball teams were supposed to be talented—up the middle. Cupid Childs and McKean were the best second baseman–shortstop combination in the league. Both could swing the bat. McKean hit .342 in 1895 and was a career .300 hitter; Cupid hit only .288 in '95, but that was an aberration. When Tebeau dropped him from the leadoff spot (to take advantage of the Crab's speed) to third in the order, Childs responded by hitting .353.

The anchor of Robison's team was the catcher, Charles Louis "Chief" Zimmer. A solid veteran, the Chief was Cy Young's personal caddy, coach, and father confessor, taking the farm boy under his wing from Young's rookie season. The Chief also made Young and the other members of the Cleveland staff better pitchers. Up until Zimmer played the position, it was common for catchers to play a full stride behind home plate. Zimmer hugged the plate, giving the pitcher a real target to throw to and giving himself an advantage to gun down runners trying to steal. Zimmer also handled the diverse styles of pitchers on the Spiders. While Young was a fireballer, George "Nig" Cuppy, Young's antithesis, threw a floater. While Young worked at a pace that gave the impression he had somewhere to be after the game, Nig was in no hurry, and his lackadaisical style frustrated hitters. With Zimmer calling the pitches, Young and Cuppy were the most formidable one-two punch in the league.

The 1895 Spiders might have finished first in the standings had not the schedule been so bad. They trailed their bitter rivals, the

Baltimore Orioles, by only three games with a week to go in the season, but the Orioles had seven games left to play, while the Spiders had only two. Cleveland split their last two games and the Orioles went 6-1. Still, the Spiders had a chance for revenge.

If the Spiders had a hardscrabble reputation, the Orioles were the gangsters of the league. The leader of the Baltimore gang was third baseman John McGraw. As dirty a player as there was, one of McGraw's milder antics was to grab hold of the belt of base runners attempting to tag up on fly balls. Inevitably the runner was easily thrown out at the plate. But Burkett, the blue-collar embodiment of the Spiders reputation, was not one to be intimidated. In the first game of the series, much to the delight of the League Park faithful, Burkett's ninth-inning double sparked a rally that propelled the Spiders to a 5–4 victory. On the strength of Burkett's four hits, Cleveland coasted to a 7–2 victory in the second game. Cy Young pitched brilliantly in allowing only one run in game three before a massive hometown crowd of nearly thirteen thousand. By the time the series moved to Baltimore, the heavily favored Orioles were stunned and down 0–3.

Orioles fans were not happy with their team's showing in Cleveland. But instead of taking out their ire on the home team, they directed it at the Spiders. Throughout game four, the visitors were showered with every imaginable projectile, including eggs, turnips, and rocks. Even though the Orioles won the game, 5–0, fans continued to assault the Spiders, now mostly with rocks and bricks as the team boarded their omnibus. "The Cleveland players had to sprawl flat on the floor of the bus to escape serious injury," wrote one Cleveland sportswriter. Undaunted by the roughnecks, Young pitched another beauty the next afternoon, and the Spiders brought Robison home the Cup.

In 1896 the Spiders again finished second, and again they played the Orioles in the Temple Cup. This time, however, Baltimore swept the series in four games. Even though the Spiders were competitive in '96, attendance at League Park began to wane. Part of the reason was baseball's rough edge. Though the demographic of fans had not changed, even the most hardened of them were becoming turned off by players' antics, brawls, and foul language. Like other owners, Robison had instituted a "Ladies Day" in an attempt to mollify rowdy crowds. The practice was not a new one. As early as 1867 the New York Knickerbockers had set aside the last Thursday of each month for the fairer sex. Later, National League franchises offered free admittance to women, as long as a man escorted them. Special sections were cordoned off for couples. Cincinnati built an enclosed entrance for women to reach their seats without walking through the crowd. Single men were not allowed in these sections. Smoking was prohibited. In Cleveland a culture of "cranklets" graced the bleachers. But even with a modicum of civility in the stands, the teams were as uncultured as ever.

But it was not only baseball's unattractiveness that kept fans from League Park. On the heels of one of the country's greatest periods of growth in manufacturing, America was plunged into an economic quagmire equaled only by the Great Depression. America simply had produced more goods and services than it could consume. For the last half of the decade, national unemployment soared above 10 percent. Homeless people, then called tramps, slept in alleyways in cities like Cleveland. The down-spiraling economy sealed the fate of the president. The once popular Grover Cleveland fell victim to a pocket-poor economy. His own Democratic Party abandoned him in 1896 and nominated William Jennings Bryan. Ohio's own William McKinley ran a campaign that capitalized on voters' financial fears with slogans like "a full dinner pail" and "cash on the barrelhead." He had struck the right note and won in a landslide general election over Bryan.

During the country's economic difficulties, railroads floundered and Robison felt the effects. His own labor force began making noises about unfair wages. Where once he dipped his hand into unlimited deep pockets, now as he rummaged there were the first signs of lint. When the railroad magnate had first bought the Forest Citys, it was more of a hobby or personal crusade than a business. But with the economic climate of the mid-1890s, such a dalliance was no longer feasible. Even with McKinley now in the Oval Office, and with him a burgeoning confidence in the economy, Robison could not weather a money pit.

As if that were not enough, Robison also had acquired the most formidable of enemies. Cleveland's powerful Protestant clergy had begun a crusade to stop Sunday baseball. Without Sunday revenue, Robison vowed to move the team from Cleveland. Rumors of the Spiders' future destination filled the daily papers. With financial pressure mounting and public opinion swaying from Robison's favor, it looked like the Spiders needed something just short of a miracle if they were going to stay in Cleveland, let alone compete for the pennant.

Luckily for Robison, in the late winter of 1897 something just short of a miracle was having a drink in a South Bend saloon.

ONCE AGAIN.

he Local Baseball Season is On in Earnest.

ng of Sockalexis, and Others.

wing's Red Men Nicely Scalped by
ebeau's Indians — Young Pitches
reat Ball and Gets Good Support
rom a Deranged Team — Local
ieycle Races — Other Sporting
ews of the Day.

YESTERDAY'S RESULTS.

eveland ... 6—Cincinnati 2
ttsburg .... 7—Louisville 4
ltimore .... 3—Brooklyn 3
w York ... 9—Washington .. 0
hicago-St. Louis—Rain.
oston-Philadelphia—Rain.

The Standing.

Clubs.	W.	L.	Pr.Ct.
iladelphia	8	1	889
ltimore	7	1	875
ncinnati	6	2	750
uisville	5	2	714
ttsburg	4	2	667
eveland	4	5	444
ooklyn	3	6	333
w York	3	5	375
ashington	2	5	286
. Louis	2	6	250
icago	2	6	2.0
ston	1	6	143

Games Today.

incinnati at Cleveland.
ouisville at Pittsburg.
t. Louis at Chicago.
altimore at Brooklyn.
ew York at Washington.
hiladelphia at Boston.

Cleveland 6, Cincinnati 2.
THE WAR CLUB.

the diamond out at League park,
Lexington and Dunham corners,
tay Tebeau, he the mighty,
the king of baseball captains,
the grass within the diamond,
od erect and called his warriors,
led his In-di-ans together,
rom his lips flowed baseball wisdom,
achings how to swipe Buck Ewing,
ipe the gang from Cincinnati,
om the town down on the Mud creek;
e metropolis that once was,
om their wigwams came the warriors,
me the swarthy baseball players,
 me McKean and Jesse Burkett,
allace, Young and Jack O'Connor,
me Great McAleer of Youngstown,
th his horse nicknamed the Charley;
ro Cuppy, late of Cuba,
ke, and Young, and Big Chief Zimmer,
d they listened to the wisdom.
, my children! My poor children!
ten to the words of warning:
ver stop 'till we have swiped 'em,
ep your eye upon the horsehide,
ot it up against the fences,
ve it over in the school yard,

Then Cy Young lined a two-bagger.
Sending Tebeau past the platter.
Burkett died at bag initial.
While big Cyrus took the third one.
Ed McKean walked down to first while
Breit paved air with good intentions.
Soxalexis hit a short one
But was out when Peltz assisted.

All of which gave the Indian's a total of
three runs, to the Red men's nothing, and
the game became too interesting to waste
time in verse, even of the rankest kind.

In the third the Reds went out in order
on three pretty plays. Zimmer got Burke's
hard foul; Wallace assisted cleverly to re-
tire Hoy and Young made a splendid stop
and throw of McPhee's hot one. Cleveland
went out in order in their half of the third,
and Cincinnati began the fourth in the
same way, and Cleveland kept up the record, Tebeau, Wallace and Young retiring
in quick succession, on an infield poke, a
fly to left and strikes, respectively.

A misunderstanding between Young and
Wallace almost gave Ritchie a base, but
Young hung on to his fly after the colli-
sion. Breitenstein got three bases on a
hit that bounded into the bleachers, but he
stayed on third while Burke and Hoy went
out.

There were two out when Sockalexis went
to first on bad ones. O'Connor singled as
the aborigine started to steal, and the latter took a desperate chance to get to third,
but he did it. O'Connor went to second on

SOCKALEXIS BREAKING FOR THIRD.

the throw, but Blake hit a foot from the
plate and was an easy out.

In the sixth nobody reached first for the

feat might easily have
of the crippled conditi
fore the victory is all
Childs' injury, susta
far more serious than
and it is a question
get back in the game
weeks.

McAleer's "Charley
the rampage, and wit
the center of Clevelan
seem to be sadly wea
appear to be yesterda
ter like McAleer him
take did Tebeau make
was as strong as eve
while Wallace need o
his conduct at third.
covered by a man in
all went swimmingly.

Interest naturally c
and the big warrio
whooped every time h
made to clever catch
throw in the field, bu
his Jonah at the bat.
had such an easy tim
on the occasion of th
pected to toy with hi
not so much of a playt
ning he struck out, m
forced to attempt a
second and sixth he h
unluckily. In the fif
balls, and was on th
knew it. A faster ma
seen.

There were one or
game that show Tebe
his men take more ch
season. The team ha
cautious about this po
led to some outside
one run was scored o
in all four stolen base

3

EARLY SPRING 1897—*Dr. Leroy Chadwick marries former fortuneteller Madame Lydia De Vere. Mrs. Chadwick, known as Cassie, would go on to swindle Cleveland bankers and other prominent citizens out of a fortune by posing as Andrew Carnegie's illegitimate daughter. At least two of her victims commit suicide. Cassie is finally caught as she tries to use securities totaling five million dollars obtained with forged signatures of Carnegie to secure a loan. She would eventually be brought to trial, one that would draw the attention of the whole world. Carnegie himself testifies that Cassie is a liar, and even a theatrical swoon by the femme-swindler-fatale at trial does not keep her from being sent to jail, where she dies one year later. Meanwhile, in March, Ohio is bursting with pride as favorite son William McKinley is inaugurated as the twenty-fifth president of the United States. Western Reserve University ends its first basketball season; James Naismith's invention of a few years before also catches on with young boys at the Broadway branch of the YMCA. On April 11 the Cleveland home for Aged Colored People opens at 284 Giddins Street, the city's first nonreligious institution run by blacks. In a front-page Easter Sunday headline the* Cleveland Plain Dealer *trumpets: "Bicycles Are All the Rage" and unabashed women in hoop skirts ride them in Public Square. Stephen Foster's "Oh! Susanna" is*

the hit song of the year, and on Cleveland's Bank Street ink-stained
newshounds rush to "Dutch" Henry's after work to listen to the tinny
piano and drink draft beer.

*   *   *   *

THE IDEA OF SIGNING AN INDIAN must have intrigued Frank
Robison, if for no other reason than to rub it in the Prussian general's face. Chris Von der Ahe, a German immigrant, was the
owner of the St. Louis Browns, or "da Prounds," as he called them.
He made his money in St. Louis beer gardens and real estate and
ran the Browns as if they were a circus act, with sideshows galore.
A giant of a man with an ego to match, he once commissioned a
larger-than-life statue of himself that was erected at the entrance to
his Sportsman's Park. At the unveiling, a St. Louis sportswriter
quipped: "Von der Ahe discovers Illinois." As far as Robison was
concerned, Von der Ahe could have his make-believe "wild west"
show and his "injun" warriors (local Indians dressed up in war
paint). If Patsy Tebeau could sign Sockalexis, Robison could parade the real deal to the plate! Maybe he could get the rookie to
pose with a tomahawk instead of a bat.

Still, he might have a hard time convincing the other owner to
go for it. And Cleveland wasn't the most racially tolerant city in the
country either. Though the Erie Canal had brought eastern fashion
and art to Cleveland, in many ways it was still a frontier town.
Selling the Indian to the players wouldn't be easy either. Hell, they

called George Cuppy "Nig" just because the guy had a dark complexion. And there was Cap Anson, the captain of the White Stockings, who wouldn't catch a ball thrown by a Negro ballplayer. In 1887, Anson led the way to "officially" ban blacks from the National League.

Tebeau wasn't thinking about publicity. From what Crab Burkett told him, the Indian could flat-out play. Burkett lived in Worcester and coached the Holy Cross baseball team when he was not playing the professional game in Cleveland. Burkett's stories of the Indian's throwing arm gave Tebeau visions of opposing players cut down at the plate. With Burkett and the Indian—two of the fastest players ever to wear a baseball uniform—in the outfield, maybe the Spiders could give Baltimore and McGraw a battle for the pennant. Tebeau wondered if the Indian had the constitution to put up with the thickheaded Irish players who just about ruled the league. But the manager knew that Sockalexis had played both football and baseball at Holy Cross. And Doc Powers had told him of a game where the Indian was ejected for nearly biting an opposing player's ear off. Then there was word of the Indian doing some damage in South Bend.

In March of 1897, Robison went to Indianapolis to meet with the other National League owners. There he fired his first salvo in his war against the clergy. He told a Cleveland sportswriter that if Sunday ball was banned he would consider moving his team to Indianapolis, where he could "get a better return on his investment." Meanwhile, through Burkett, Tebeau sent a contract to the Indian at Holy Cross. According to newspaper reports, the Indian signed the contract while still in Worcester. Yet for reasons unknown, he packed his bags and followed Doc Powers to South Bend. According to university records, he enrolled in the prep school of Notre Dame, where his schedule included classes in Christian doctrine, algebra, French, composition, and spelling. School records also state that he had begun to practice with the university's baseball team, and that he played on an intramural basketball team (not familiar with the game, he once scored two points for the opposing team). On February 13, 1897, *The Scholastic,* the Notre Dame student magazine, told of his arrival: "A new candidate for centre-field, Sockalexis, came out for the first time on Thursday last. His batting, fielding and throwing were remarkable."

What's confusing about the whole matter is that if newspaper accounts are correct, then Sockalexis turned down Tebeau's offer of a two-thousand-dollar National League contract to attend Notre Dame. Although Notre Dame was gaining a national reputation at the time, the university was nowhere near the powerful institution it is today. It's extremely doubtful that the school could offer anything in the way of incentive to match the National League money. An 1897 Notre Dame ledger book shows an entry on February 10 for Louis F. Sockalexis from Old Town, Maine. After the listings of entrance fee, board, and tuition there is the notation "Special" that indicates, according to a college sports researcher, Sockalexis was the equivalent of today's grant-in-aid or scholarship student. The only charges on his ledger were for socks

($1.50), ink ($.10), and books ($9.60). There is the possibility that Powers knew of leagues in northern Indiana for ballplayers to make money, but there is no record to support that theory. Though the situation is confusing, very shortly after his arrival at South Bend, the point becomes moot.

One evening after practice, Sockalexis and a Notre Dame teammate decided to take in the local color. They spent a good part of the afternoon at Old Oscar McGoggins', a saloon favored by South Bend's working class. After squeezing the last drop of bourbon from Old Oscar, the pair moved on to an establishment of questionable morals run by one "Popcorn" Jenny. One story of that night intimated that Popcorn took exception to providing her services to a "red man." In reaction to the lack of hospitality, the Indian and his pal decided to rearrange the establishment's furniture. The upholstered chairs and loveseats, they concluded, would look better on the outside of the building. Of course, the quickest way to perform the task was to throw them out of the windows.

While the impromptu interior decoration was proceeding, the local authorities were called. One of the policemen made a rather unflattering reference to the Indian's heritage, which elicited a kind of sign language response. Actually it was more of a punch. The Indian and his pal were finally subdued and carted off to the police station. Despite the egregiousness of the incident, all might have eventually been forgiven had not a *South Bend Tribune* reporter been somehow apprised of the situation. The lead story in the next day's paper drew the attention of the Reverend Father Andrew

Morrisey, the president of Notre Dame University, and the Indian and his pal were promptly asked to leave the school. Under the headline "Expelled From Notre Dame," this news story ran the following day:

> The two disorderly drunks arrested yesterday afternoon were students from the University of Notre Dame where the news was carried by telephone at an early hour last evening. On hearing of the conduct of the two young men the university authorities ordered their effects packed and sent to them with the information that their presence at Notre Dame was no longer desired. Both were released last night.
>
> One of them was Sockalexis, the noted young Indian base ball player, who was recently signed to play with the Cleveland national league club after the close of the season at Notre Dame, where he said he desired to finish his studies. He left the city over the Lake Shore railroad at 11:42 presumably for Cleveland, Ohio. The other young man was one of the most popular students at the university and stood high in social circles in this city. For the sake of what he has been and what he may still be his name is not published. The prompt action of the university authorities in expelling these young men should be a warning to others inclined to overstep the bounds of propriety.

The other student was Edme Chassaing, an established star on Indiana's amateur baseball circuit. The article's omission of Chassaing's name—and the prominence of Sockalexis's—speaks volumes of the inherent racism of the day. The story also, perhaps, clears up some of the confusion. If the information is correct, Sockalexis thought his studies important enough to delay his start in the National League. He could have done both, missing only about a month of the professional season.

The news traveled fast. A wire obtained by the *Cleveland Plain Dealer* read in part: "The faculty of Notre Dame University today took summary action by expelling Sockalexis, the famous Indian ball player, who was enrolled as a student." Doc Powers wired Tebeau. The Spiders' captain took the next train to South Bend, paid the Indian's fine, and presented him with a contract for the coming season. In the meantime, Notre Dame did its part to hasten the Indian's departure. According to a student account ledger dated March 19, 1897, the university gave or lent the Indian $10 in cash for a train ticket to Cleveland, $3 for "hack fare," and listed an unpaid amount of $9.60 for textbooks, making the total amount due $22.60. (An addendum to the ledger, dated July 16, 1897, lists the receipt of a post office order in the full amount of $22.60 from Sockalexis, prompting one university official to remark that the former Notre Damer was an "honest injun.") Though the Indian's departure from Notre Dame was acrimonious and sordid, his arrival in Cleveland was nothing short of sensational.

The headline on the sports page of the *Cleveland Plain Dealer* read: "The Great Sockalexis Is Here." You could almost feel the heat

from the sportswriters rubbing their hands in delight. He was
"Chief Sock-it-on-the-nose" in one sports story, "Big-man-sock-it-
to-'em" in another. This poem written by C. A. Conrad greeted the
Indian in a Cleveland paper:

Said Pat Tebeau to the score-card man,
"Tell me, please sir, if you can,
Is there room on our batting list
for my latest find, Sockalexis?
The score-card man took his pencil out,
In his fertile mind he had no doubt,
That he readily could with becoming grace,
Compress the name in a very small space.

"Let's see: two, four, six, eight, ten:
Suppose we cut out just a few,
And then we'll see what I can do."

Hadn't he done such things before?
Guess he could do it at least once more.
Remembering well that he'd some years back
Transformed "McGuillicuddy" into plain "Mack."

He scanned the name and mused awhile,
"How is this?" An artless smile.
He has written it "Sock." Pat grinned a grin,
And said, "You'd better try again."

"Won't do? Well now I do declare,
then why not make an even pair?
So I'll add the s. How that is it."
He had written it "Socks." Quote Patsy, "nit."

Neither "Alex" or Aleck" the captain would suit
And Alexis was thrown in to boot,
Said Pat, "It's a blooming, bleeding shame
But the fellow will have to change his name."

But perhaps there was another reason for the use of a homonym, one born out of frustration—"Sockalexis" was just not Indian-sounding enough. It did not stir passion and evoke an era and a place like the names Crazy Horse and Sitting Bull. It didn't bring to mind the legendary battles of Little Big Horn or Wounded Knee. The Penobscot had not fought the white man for over a century. In fact, by the late 1800s there were no "full-blooded" members of the tribe. Chances are that the name was a corruption of "St. Alexis"; French Jesuit missionaries had converted most Penobscots by the mid-1700s. There was also an inland Penobscot tribe called Sokoki, the name meaning "far away," that could have been the genesis of Sockalexis. But if the name was not romantic enough for sportswriters, the history of Sockalexis's people was every bit as sad as that of any of the frontier tribes.

The Indian's arrival had everyone in Cleveland talking baseball. From the stately homes on Euclid Avenue to the Angle, the Irish parish ghetto of St. Malachi's church, from dockworkers on the shore of the great Lake Erie to passengers on the elegant side-wheel steamers that motored up and down the Cuyahoga River, discussion of the Indian and the upcoming Spiders season was seemingly on everyone's lips. Though the topic had people dreaming of luxuriating on warm summer afternoons at the ballpark, the reality was that it was still March in Cleveland. A cold, wet snow wrapped the city in a runny white.

In 1897 the Cleveland Athletic Club (no relation to the CAC founded in 1908) acted as the spring training site for the Spiders. It was located at 927 Euclid Avenue and, for its time, it was one of the country's best facilities. In the early 1890s the club sponsored "exhibition" boxing matches between the likes of John L. Sullivan, Jim Corbett, and Bob Fitzsimmons. Later in the decade the club held sanctioned matches. On its indoor track trained some of the land's best milers. The club was also home to bicycle races and its members helped perpetuate that craze in Cleveland during the 1890s. In addition to the Spiders' presence, the club also sponsored its own "gentlemen's team." The membership of the club was a who's who of Cleveland's elite, and Robison had a great deal of influence.

Though the weather wasn't the least bit cooperative, Tebeau was aching to see how the rookies, especially Sockalexis, could perform. So despite the bitter cold, on April 4 the manager marched most of the team outside to practice. It was too cold for the stars: Young, Cuppy, Childs, Burkett, and others stayed in the steam-heated gymnasium of the athletic club. With the wind blowing off Lake Erie, it was hard to tell the difference between early April and late January. The brown grass crunched underneath the players' spikes, and crystallized breath smoked from their mouths like steam from a locomotive. Tebeau and fifteen or so Spiders, along with three local men who played league ball in the city, warmed up as best they could.

Of the complement of Spiders, at least nine were rookies, like Sock, or marginal veterans trying to secure a position on the team. Tebeau decided to field the makeshift roster into two squads and play a practice game. It wasn't a fair match. Tebeau placed all of his regulars on one team and the untested lot on the other. About six hundred cranks and every sportswriter in Cleveland watched Sockalexis as he jogged out to his position in right field. The *Cleveland Plain Dealer* recorded the event: "Sockalexis was the most observed man on the field. . . . He had to stand about as much 'kidding' from the bleachers as the average outsider."

A local scribe pointed out to the Spiders manager the disparity of the two teams. Tebeau answered by saying that the game would feature the "Papooses" (rookies) against the "Indians" (veterans). Tebeau had never really liked the team's name. "Spiders" might have been a shade better than "Beaneaters," but the moniker was no longer representative of the Cleveland team. The Hooligans or the Brawlers would have been more like it.

It's only a guess that Tebeau's choice of a new nickname was because of the guy pounding his mitt in right, but it's a good guess. In those years, professional baseball franchises didn't have official team names. More often than not, the team's nickname was born out of the imagination of the local sportswriters, for example the Trolley Dodgers and the Beaneaters. Sometimes the team was named simply after the color of the uniform or socks: Reds, White Stockings, Browns. Still others used the name of their best player, as in the case of the Cleveland Naps of the early 1900s; Hall of Fame player Napoleon LaJoie was their star.

A *Sporting News* column called "Cleveland Chatter," dated March 22, 1897, was perhaps the first published mention of "Indians" as the new name for the Cleveland team: "There is no feature of the signing of Sockalexis more gratifying than the fact that his presence on the team will result in relegating to obscurity the title of 'Spiders' by which the team has been handicapped for several seasons, to give place to the more significant name 'Indians.'" Regardless of whether the *Sporting News* was first, for as long as Sockalexis played for Cleveland, they were unanimously called the Indians by both the press and the fans.

On the practice field Tebeau told sportswriters that the rookies might as well face the stiffest competition if they wanted to show they could play in the National League. He told the veteran pitchers, however, to lay off the junk and throw only "straight balls." Even in the 1890s the curveball, or the drop pitch as it was then called, caused the legs of rookie batters to shake like chicken fat. Though the Indian garnered all onlookers' attention, Tebeau was more interested in John Pappalau, the lanky rookie pitcher from Albany, New York, and a teammate of Sockalexis at Holy Cross. The manager had a foreboding feeling about the state of his pitching staff. Most of his uneasiness grew from the poor mound display against Baltimore in the prior season's Temple Cup series. Cy Young's arm had look tired, and there was no telling if it would come back or not. Throughout the Temple Cup series, only Nig Cuppy pitched well, and in only one game: the fourth against Baltimore at League Park. Cuppy had dueled Joe Corbett, the younger brother of "Gentleman" Jim, then the heavyweight champ, through six scoreless innings before he tired. But by then the Spiders—or, as they were now being called, the Indians—had all but given up, down three games to none. With Cuppy on the bench, Baltimore wrapped up the Cup with a 3–0 victory.

Although with not nearly the publicity surrounding Sockalexis, Pappalau was highly touted. Interest on the sportswriters' part was strictly one of osmosis. He was signed the same day as the Indian. But Tebeau was more pragmatic. He saw raw talent. At a husky six feet, Pappalau was a power pitcher. Though in those days there wasn't any way to scientifically measure pitch speed, the consensus of baseball historians is that the fastest pitchers of that era, like Young and Amos Rusie of the Giants, threw ninety miles per hour plus. Pappalau, it was said, was as fast as the best. Still, as much as the manager tried to concentrate on his rookie pitcher, there was something almost magnetic about right field.

With the raw day and the weighty ball, Pappalau had things on his side. For the first couple of innings the vets couldn't hit the ball out of the infield. They managed to scratch out only a couple of hits that were actually balls misplayed by the rookie and ringer fielders. On the mound for the veterans was Mike McDermott, a scrawny junk baller recently acquired from Louisville, Kentucky. With Tebeau's edict of no curveballs, McDermott was little more than a batting-practice pitcher, and the rookies teed off on him.

Sockalexis roped a couple of shots to the gaps and glided in easily for two doubles. He also beat out two infield choppers for singles. But it was one play in right that had those in attendance believing something special was happening that spring at League Park.

A veteran had finally got hold of a Pappalau fastball, and the drive was high and deep to right-center. With the crack of the bat, the Indian was in full gallop. The ball was far over his head, too far to be caught, or at least it looked that way at first. Yet there seemed to occur a slowing of time, at least for all earthly moving bodies but the Indian's. It was almost as though his graceful footfalls were the only sound heard in the slow-motion surroundings. The ball seemed to hang as though strung from the cold, gray Cleveland sky.

During his baseball life, there were moments on the diamond when Sockalexis seemed propelled by a force other than just athletic talent, when it seemed he was not wearing a uniform, when his hand did not wear a glove, moments that were misty and dreamlike. In the world of his ancestors, a Penobscot boy would lead the hunting party deep into the Maine woods. He would be among the fastest of the tribe, a winner of races watched by Penobscot elders. Pine branches would whip his face and chest as he flushed out the game and fowl. There was oneness in purity between the boy and beast, a natural predatory order—the quickest would conquer. As the baseball arched high over Sockalexis, the playing field became the woods of his childhood. He heard no sound, save the brush of branches. There was a moment when those who witnessed the play did not believe their senses. The ball must have landed well beyond his grasp. But the Indian's body language told them that the catch had been made.

The following day a freezing rain fell on Cleveland, and all the players practiced indoors at the athletic club. Tebeau ordered some laps on the track, one of the best indoor running facilities in the country. Some of the veterans, Chief Zimmer especially, had added some winter pounds and spent time in the steam room. Others tossed medicine balls and worked out on the parallel bars. It was a good day to start the tournament, the manager thought.

The handball tournament was an annual event that Tebeau had both organized and won every year. As was custom, Tebeau would first play the rookies, a kind of baptismal right of passage. Pappalau was the first to be led to the altar. The manager had the rookie hitting more walls than handballs. After not winning a single point, Pappalau slunk to the back of the audience, hoots and howls serenading him on his defeated march. Sockalexis stood passively as the howls grew louder. Tebeau wiped the perspiration from his face with a towel and searched those players gathered around the court for his next victim. Like Pilate yielding to the crowd's cry for Barabbas, Tebeau shrugged and crooked a beckoning finger toward Sockalexis.

Whether Sock had ever played handball before that day is not known, and after the first few volleys it looked as though he had not. Tebeau's cagey tactics had the rookie off balance, and the manager easily racked up the first few points of the game. Sensing another rookie's defeat, the crowd grew louder. Playing to his following, Tebeau confidently swatted a hard serve against the wall. Handball, however, is basically a game of quickness, and here Sockalexis was without peer. As his focus narrowed, the sights and sounds around him disappeared. He dove at the hard rubber ball and in one motion slapped it past his captain. The jeers from the crowd stilled, replaced by a few whistles of disbelief. The game was on.

As the rest of the team drew closer to witness the display of athletic prowess, Tebeau grew frustrated, more times than not lying face first on the court and slapping the wood floor with each missed volley. Tebeau didn't score another point. After the winning serve again left Tebeau sprawled on the court, Sockalexis offered a hand to help him up. Embarrassed, the captain swatted it away.

The next day, when two-man teams were formed and wagers placed, Sockalexis's name was not among the list of players. He watched the finals of the tournament with a kind of silent resignation as Tebeau and his partner, "Roady" Wallace, won. In the pecking order of major league clubhouses, rookies, like children, were to be seen and not heard. Beating the captain and manager at his own game was perhaps not the best way to ingratiate oneself with the team. When you add the attending publicity that surrounded his arrival and the inherent animosity toward his race, and in spite of the fact that the team had been renamed for him, Sockalexis wasn't exactly warmly welcomed to the team.

To his credit, Tebeau cared little about the color of a player's skin. He was all for the signing of Sockalexis—his long trip to South Bend is a testament to that. He was, pure and simple, a baseball man, and as one, his only prejudice was toward those who kept him from winning games. If the manager held any hard feelings toward the Indian, it was only because of a wounded ego, and that lasted only until he got back to the business of running the team. That wouldn't take long. If the Indian fulfilled his potential—and judging by early returns Tebeau had no doubt he would—the manager would have the freedom to make some changes he had mulled over during the off-season.

In 1895, Roderick "Roady" Wallace was the starting pitcher in thirty games for Cleveland. In that Temple Cup year, his record was a tepid 12–14. The manager thought his pal would never be anything but a mediocre pitcher but was convinced that, with enough at bats, Wallace was a .300 hitter. He had experimented with Wallace playing the outfield part-time in 1896. As he walked from the court, Tebeau glanced at the Indian. If things worked out like he hoped, Wallace would play this season at third, and right field would be manned by the rookie who played a damn fine game of handball.

It's doubtful the Indian had any worries about making the team. Though insecure and immature in many ways (for example, the incident at Notre Dame), he had supreme confidence in his athletic abilities. The day after the handball tournament, the manager made the rookie's place on the team official. "The Cleveland ax will be very slow in falling," Tebeau told a sports reporter from the *Plain Dealer*. "Not a Cleveland player will be released until June, if any are then." Still, the Indian wasn't sure where he fit into Tebeau's plans. He would quickly find out.

As the team readied for exhibition games to be held in

Columbus, Louisville, and Grand Rapids, Michigan, as tune-ups for the regular season, Tebeau told the Indian to pack his equipment for the trip. He was to start in right field for the regular club in the first road game against Columbus.

At that same time, Robison was in Cincinnati meeting with the Red Stockings president, John T. Brush. The question among cranks was not if the team would eventually leave Cleveland, but to which city they would move. Detroit, Louisville, Milwaukee, and Buffalo were just some of the destinations mentioned in news articles. Robison's trip to Cincinnati immediately fueled rumors of the team heading there. According to Robison, the fate of the team hung on whether or not the clergy would allow Sunday games. Robison had insisted that he couldn't make a profit without a full weekend of play. But Robison knew that neither side of the battle, himself nor the clergy, held the deciding vote. The final decision lay with the paying customers. If enough Clevelanders wanted the games played, even the most influential minister couldn't and wouldn't stop them. As a sporting gentleman, Robison knew that his battle with the clergy was nothing more than a game of high stakes poker. All the chips were on the table, and he viewed the Indian like a matching ace in the hole.

Burkett and Childs were the only proven veterans in the lineup when the Cleveland Indians took the field in Columbus. The day was raw, and some of the regulars groused that it was just too cold to play. Even Tebeau decided to don a winter coat and help man the turnstile instead of first base. Perhaps he wanted to make sure the Indians received a fair count at the gate. After all, the manager of the Columbus club was his older brother, George "White Wings" Tebeau, and despite the angelic nickname, George was known to have quick hands—and not just when playing third base.

Sockalexis didn't seem to notice the cold. Coming from Maine, where winters start sometime after the Fourth of July, Columbus was almost balmy. He went three for four at the plate and was robbed of a hit when Charlie Babb, the Columbus third baseman, snagged a sizzling liner over the bag. Sock cost his team a run in the seventh inning when he stumbled over a ground ball base hit; the runner stretched the single into three bases on the Indian's gaff and scored on a sacrifice fly. But with the score tied 3–3 in the ninth, Sockalexis saved a potential run with a perfect throw to second, gunning down George Tebeau as he tried for a double. The game ended in a deadlock as a cold rain began to fall.

The Indian sat alone on the train to Dayton, staring out the window at the passing countryside. The rain had continued throughout the previous night and into the next day, and the second game against Columbus was canceled. One of the players had hung the nickname "Chief" on the Indian. Someone handed the Chief a cigar, which he lit with a stick match. He exhaled a blue-white plume, adding to the miasma of smoke in the train car. He could get used to this, he thought: traveling the country, playing ball, beat the reservation with a baseball bat. Though the guys weren't exactly friendly, he hoped that he would eventually be accepted. Talent was the great equalizer. He knew that from Holy

Cross. Those college boys had been cool to him too, until he started to rope liners all over the field. When Holy Cross won, which they did more often than not, the students would throw a party. All the players were guests of honor, and Sock was at the top of the list. The team would warm to him, the Indian thought. Hell, they'd be buying him drinks before the regular season started.

As the team's train rumbled toward Columbus, Robison boarded one for New York to attend the National League owners meeting. That week the Cleveland team's fate was debated in papers across the country. Detroit and Louisville had special interests in Cleveland's situation. Both cities had professional teams, but not ones that played in the National League, the plum circuit. The owners of those two teams were plotting to take over Cleveland's spot should Robison opt not to move but simply shut down operations. A Louisville paper reported that the president of the Detroit team had offered Dr. T. Hunt Stucky, the owner of the Louisville club, "thousands of dollars" for his franchise. But the conspirators were delving in fantasy. For any deal that would leave Robison empty-handed was about as realistic as an all-black team playing in the National League.

In New York, Robison met with most of the National League presidents at the Fifth Avenue Hotel. These meetings often resembled an underworld summit. In attendance along with Robison were Von der Ahe and Brush. But what gave the meeting its shady appearance was the presence of New York Giants owner Andrew Freedman, whom baseball aficionado Bill James once described as "George Steinbrenner on Quaaludes with a touch of Al Capone."

Freedman was half realtor, half gangster. In his obituary the *New York Times* called him the "power behind the throne" of crooked Tammany Hall boss Richard Crocker.

Like Steinbrenner's early years in New York, Freedman's antics were constant fodder for the press. One article in the *New York Journal* described a forfeited wager by the magnate, and the ensuing barroom brawl: "Early in the season of 1896, Bert Dasher, a representative of the Hoyt & McKee theatrical firm, says he made a bet with Andy the Giants would not finish one, two, three. The Giants landed far below Dasher's prophecy, and when he asked Freedman to settle the claims the magnate repudiated the wager. The pair met later in the bar of the Fifth Avenue hotel, where Freedman again opened hostilities by harpooning Dasher with a $2 cane." The story went on to say that the pair wrestled at the crowded bar, sending a bowl of "parched corn and cracker" flying. At one point during the struggle, Freedman found himself face first in an "ornate cuspidor." As Freedman wiped the expectorate from his eyes, he realized he was missing his diamond pin. "During the racket the magnate's diamond horse shoe broke from its moorings in his four-in-hand tie and became a derelict. Freedman, at the time, did not note the absence of his jewelry, but when the fight was over and he had wiped the debris from his eyes he accused Frank Lane, an actor, of having stolen the bauble. This charge would have resulted in another fight had not the crowd taken pity on the magnate," the *Journal* concludes.

Not all of the magnates gathered in New York were of Freedman's cloth. Harry Von der Horst was known as one of the game's true gentlemen. Honest about his limited knowledge of baseball, Von der Horst hired Ned Hanlon to run the team. Von der Horst was known to wear a button that said: ASK HANLON. But despite his proclaimed naïveté, handing the reins over to Hanlon was a shrewd business move. Baltimore baseball historian James H. Bready once wrote of Hanlon: "In judging men, and swapping ballplayers, Hanlon had moments akin to clairvoyance."

Though the press waited in abeyance for word of Cleveland's baseball future, Robison uncharacteristically stayed mum on the issue. He would wait and see how the Indian experiment worked out before saying any more. So far things were moving along nicely. Hell, the *Sporting News* was already writing about the rookie. A sportswriter from that sheet asked Robison what he thought of Sockalexis's chances of making the team. "He's a fine young man, a fine ball player," Robison answered. He wanted to say, Hell yes, he'll play! Do you take me for an idiot? Those loud-mouthed ministers whose Sunday sermons were published every Monday in the *Plain Dealer* could rail all they wanted. With the Indian in right field, cranks would be hanging off the Payne Avenue streetcar on Sunday—despite the fact that he had raised the fare from two to three cents.

In Dayton, Sockalexis went two-for-four at the plate. Both of the hits were clean line drives. But once again it was his play in the field that wowed those in attendance. He had two outfield assists, throwing out runners trying to advance on fly balls. One of these throws came in the eighth inning as Dayton tried to mount a rally. The Dayton player tagged third base on a fairly deep fly to right and streaked toward home as the Indian made the catch. The throw was in the catcher's mitt before the runner had a chance to begin his slide. The rally was over, and players on both teams shook their heads in amazement.

Again the team took to the rails. The rhythmic thump of the tracks lulled the players to sleep, except for Sockalexis, who stared into the blackness outside the train window. That afternoon's game in Dayton had been played in raw, wet weather and lasted only seven innings. He had gone two-for-four at the plate in the Cleveland rout of the Western League team. Though not his best effort with the bat, he made one hit count for a run as he flashed his speed in stealing second, then blazed around third to score a run on a single. The Indian's speed was as impressive as his throwing arm. It was almost impossible to throw him out on an infield chopper, and he was a cinch to score from second on any base hit.

Sportswriters that season lamented the bygone days of the stolen base. Chief Zimmer's innovation of crowding the back of home plate had caught on with other catchers in the league, cutting the distance of the throw-out on attempted steals. Plus, umpires gave pitchers much leeway on balk moves. In 1895 the pitching rubber had been enlarged to twenty-four by six inches, which enhanced deception in the windup and gave pitchers a better platform from which to push off. None of this affected Sockalexis. He was faster than any catcher's throw. He seemed to know what the pitcher was thinking.

The train pulled into Ann Arbor as the sun peeked through the high white Michigan sky. The sun did little to warm the still winter air as the team took the field. In the grandstand, cranks huddled for warmth. Something there in the stands drew Sock's attention. A small group of Potawatomi Indians had ventured from the nearby reservation to watch him play. The ubiquitous sign still hung in stores and saloons: No Dogs or Indians. Sockalexis knew that to the white man—the cranks, the owners, even his fellow players—he was a novelty, a side show, a cigar store carving. He knew that if he couldn't throw a baseball like an arrow shot from a bow, if he wasn't a step faster than everyone else, if the ball didn't jump off his bat with the ferocity it did, he would be in a bateau pushing logs down the Penobscot River, wearing the white man's cast-off clothing, drinking cheap whiskey. As the Indian stood in right, in the stands the Potawatomi cheered. In a century of humiliation and loss at the hands of whites, one of their own had won a victory.

While Sockalexis went one-for-four that day, the Senate of the United States put the final touches on the Indian Appropriations Bill, which would allow the further acquisition of mineral-rich reservation lands. In Montana, a Cheyenne chief gathered his tribe and plotted their escape from the Tongue River reservation. In Michigan, the Indian boarded a train to Louisville and the start of a baseball summer.

AT LENGTH, AT LAST

The Indians Hang One Little Scalp at Their Belts.

The War Club Wielded Vigorously

Tebeau Has a Battle With an Umpire Which Puts Him in Fighting Trim—Out of Last Place—The Lajoie and Connolly Fight — Arrangements for the C. W. C. Races —General Sporting News.

YESTERDAY'S RESULTS.

Cleveland ...12—St. Louis 4
Louisville .... 3—Chicago 2
Baltimore ... 5—New York 3
Philadelphia . 5—Brooklyn 2
Washington.... 3—Boston 8
Cincinnati-Pittsburg—Rain.

The Standing.

Clubs.	W.	L.	Pr.Ct.
Philadelphia	7	1	875
Baltimore	7	1	875
Cincinnati	6	1	857
Louisville	5	1	833
Pittsburg	3	2	600
Brooklyn	3	5	375
Washington	2	4	333
St. Louis	2	4	333
New York	2	5	286
Chicago	2	6	250
Cleveland	1	5	167
Boston	1	6	143

Today's Games.

Cleveland at St. Louis.
Chicago at Louisville.
Pittsburg at Cincinnati.
New York at Baltimore.
Brooklyn at Philadelphia.
Boston at Washington.

Special to the Plain Dealer.

Cleveland 12—St. Louis 4.

ST. LOUIS, Mo., April 30.—Pat Tebeau struck his gait this afternoon and started on his long journey toward the championship. The Spiders played horse with the Browns and actually made them look like a lot of babies.

After yesterday's game Pat had a show down with Umpire McDonald. The Cleveland chieftain did not hesitate to tell the man of the indicator what he thought of him, and they came near having a game of fisticuffs. Later in the evening McDonald hunted Tebeau up at his hotel and wanted to have it out there and then. Pat could not see what the use of fighting off the field was, and would not make it a go. The little affair seemed to have thrown the man many battles back to his old stride and

Dunn—O'Connor 1. Wild pitches—Willson 1. Time—2:05. Umpire—McDonald.

Philadelphia 5—Brooklyn 2.

PHILADELPHIA, April 30.—Philadelphia defeated Brooklyn today in a pretty battle of pitchers McMahon, late of Baltimore, pitched his first game of the season, as did also Wheeler. In no inning were more than two hits made off either. The fielding of both was first-class. Attendance 4,529. Score:

Philadelphia.	A.B.	R.	H.	O.	A.	E.
Cooley, c. f.	4	0	0	2	0	0
Hallman, 2b	4	1	2	2	2	1
Geier, r. f.	5	2	2	1	0	0
Delehanty, l. f.	4	0	2	2	0	0
Cross, 3b	3	0	0	3	2	1
Clements, c.	4	0	1	3	3	0
Boyle, 1b	4	0	0	10	0	0
Gillen, s. s.	2	1	1	3	7	0
Wheeler, p.	3	1	0	1	1	0
Totals	33	5	8	27	15	2

Brooklyn.	A.B.	R.	H.	O.	A.	E.
Griffin, c. f.	2	0	1	5	0	0
Jones, r. f.	4	0	0	2	0	0
Anderson, l. f.	4	0	2	1	0	0
Shindle, 3b	3	0	1	1	2	1
Lachance, 1b	3	1	0	8	1	0
Canavan, 2b	3	1	0	0	3	0
G. Smith, s. s.	4	0	0	5	2	0
Grim, c.	4	0	0	4	1	0
McMahon, p.	3	0	1	1	2	0
Totals	30	2	5	27	11	2

Philadelphia ... 0 0 0 2 0 1 0 1 0—5
Brooklyn ...... 0 2 0 0 0 0 0 0 0—2

Earned runs—Philadelphia 2. Two-base hits—Gillen, Shindle. Stolen base—Lachance. Double play—By Wheeler 3, to Boyle. First base on balls—Off Wheeler 5, off McMahon 3. Hit by pitcher—Hallman. Struck out—By Wheeler 3, by McMahon 4. Wild pitch—McMahon. Left on bases—Philadelphia 7, Brooklyn 6. Sacrifice hits—Cross, Wheeler. Time—1:55. Umpire—Emslie.

Baltimore 5—New York 3.

BALTIMORE, April 30.—The Champions took the second game of the series from the Giants much as they pleased, although the game at times looked close. In the fourth Keeler made a phenomenal catch of Beckley's long hit, but the next one in his garden was from Seymour's bat, and bounding over the fence scored the only home run made this season. Score:

Baltimore.	A.B.	R.	H.	O.	A.	E.
Quinn, 3b	4	0	0	2	3	1
Keeler, r. f.	4	3	3	4	0	0
Jennings, s. s	4	0	1	3	3	0
Kelley, l. f.	4	0	1	4	0	0
Doyle, 1b	3	0	0	10	1	0
Stenzel, c. f.	3	1	1	2	0	0
Reitz, 2b	3	1	1	1	2	0
Clark, c.	3	0	1	1	1	0
Hoffer, p.	3	0	0	1	0	0
Totals	31	5	8	27	10	1

New York.	A.B.	R.	H.	O.	A.	E.
Van Haltren, c. f.	5	0	1	3	0	0
Tiernan, r. f.	4	0	1	3	0	0
Joyce, 3b	4	0	1	1	1	0
Gleason, 2b	3	1	2	4	3	0
Beckley, 1b	4	0	0	7	1	0
Seymour, l. f.	4	2	2	1	0	2
Stafford, s. s.	4	0	1	2	2	0
Warner, c.	3	0	0	3	1	0
Sullivan, p.	4	0	0	1	0	0
Totals	35	3	8	24	9	2

Baltimore .... 1 0 0 1 2 1 0 0 *—5
New York..... 0 0 0 1 0 2 0 0 0—3

Earned runs—New York 2, Baltimore 2. Two-base hits—Seymour. Three-base hit

---

4

LATE SPRING 1897—*As the weather in Cleveland warms, the city mourns the death of eight workers killed in an explosion in the new water works tunnel—the blast occurred more than a mile from shore in Lake Erie. In the* Plain Dealer, *Clevelanders read of the war between Turkey and Greece; led by Prince Constantine, the Greeks attack the Turk army in Thessaly. William Randolph Hearst hires writer Stephen Crane to be his war correspondent; Crane's The* Red Badge of Courage, *published in 1895, is a popular read in Cleveland. According to newspapers, the famous Hatfield and McCoy feud in Wheeling, West Virginia, ends with the marriage of Aaron Hatfield, the nephew of "Devil Anse" Hatfield, the outlaw king of Logan Country, and Mary McCoy, the daughter of Randolph McCoy, the patriarch of that clan. In Cleveland, parks, especially Brookside Park, become popular gathering places; the Great Western Band performs the first Sunday concert in Gordon Park. A young Cleveland inventor by the name of Archie C. Walker introduces an "aerial torpedo" that he claims can fly a distance of nine miles and carry a load of dynamite. In Cleveland markets, milk sells for six cents a quart, ham for thirteen cents a pound, eggs "strictly fresh" for twelve cents a dozen. Ayers sarsaparilla is a popular tonic on the shelves of apothecaries. An estimated fifty thousand Clevelanders own bicycles, and the newfan-*

73

gled "built for two" bike is a best-selling model. A specially equipped wagon is available to water Millionaires Row on Euclid Avenue, to keep the street dust down; the service costs two dollars a month, and the water is shut off when it passes houses whose owners fall behind on payment.

* * * *

THE GAME OF BASEBALL had gone through something of a metamorphosis by the late 1890s. Dimensions and rules were then in place that would form the modern game, the most notable being the distance between the pitching rubber and home plate, which in 1893 was lengthened from fifty feet to sixty feet, six inches. Though the extra ten feet, six inches was a huge advantage to the batter, it caused a subtler and more lasting change in baseball overall. The "scientific game" was born. With the pitcher moved back from home plate, runs were scratched out with bunts and stolen bases. Baltimore's "Wee" Willie Keeler summed up the era with his now famous edict: "Hit 'em where they ain't."

Still, baseball was in its adolescence, and like most teenagers it got away with what it could. Slight of hand, even outright cheating, was in vogue. Baseballs were hidden in the long outfield grass. When a drive seemed destined to split the gap, outfielders would magically come up with a ball and throw the runner out at second. With only one umpire then, players, especially John McGraw, would often stretch a double into a triple by cutting across the infield from first to third. In Philadelphia an elaborate set of wires and levers connected the dugout to a perch in center field. There, a home team scout relayed the opposing catcher's signs.

Perhaps the most adolescent aspect of the game was the players' temperaments. Crab Burkett was ejected and fined at least a half dozen times during the 1897 season for his colorful use of language, mostly directed toward umpires. In one game, most of the Cleveland team was arrested in a dispute with an ump. After a disputed call, Burkett, Patsy Tebeau, Jimmy McAleer, and other Cleveland players surrounded the umpire, taunting him with epithets. McAleer purportedly punched the ump, prompting the warrants to be issued. Players like Burkett and McGraw were known for kicking the umpire to punctuate their argument, and their antics, more often then not, incited the fans.

In Pittsburgh that season some five hundred cranks, spurred on by an unpopular call, followed the umpire from the field into the clubhouse. In a questionable display of judgment, the ump took a swing at a leader of the band of fans. A row erupted, with fans taking turns pummeling the official. A few Pittsburgh players emerged from the locker room brandishing bats and threatening to brain any fan that didn't move back, their hubris born more out of self-defense that any act of heroism. The standoff remained tense, verging on a full-scale riot, until members of the Allegheny police force arrived and were able to escort the ump to safety.

Umpires could be just as bad as the players. Later that 1897 season, umpire Jack Sheridan responded to a Pirates pitcher's taunt by punching the player in the face. The pitcher, "Pink" Hawley, then knocked Sheridan out cold for a full ten minutes. After being revived by a cold compress, Sheridan and the game continued. In Cincinnati a fan threw a beer glass at umpire Tim Hurst. Hurst picked the glass up and hurled it back into the stands, seriously injuring a fan. Hurst was promptly arrested. Not surprisingly, turnover at the umpire position was swift. Some fifty-nine different men umpired during the 1896 season.

Sockalexis was not intimidated by the ribald nature of the National League. His background was one of everyday hardships, of poverty that swallowed even the toughest loggers like a swamped bateau in the rapids of the Penobscot River. He was schooled under the austere rigidity of the Jesuits, who were known to raise a hand every now and then to inattentive students. At Holy Cross his reputation as roughneck football player almost equaled his reputation as a gifted baseball star. There were several newspaper accounts of his vicious tackles on opposing players. When he was arrested in South Bend, the news account said that it took "several policemen" to subdue Sockalexis. Standing nearly six feet tall and weighing in at around two hundred pounds, he towered over most of the other players.

Beyond his physical toughness, by the time Sockalexis arrived in the National League he had also endured years of racist attitudes in white institutions. His skin was not only a darker hue, it was as tough as the horsehide on the baseballs he smacked around the field. But though his exterior might have been life-hardened, on the inside, like any rookie, he needed to be accepted.

Teams of Sock's era bonded out of a kind of necessity. Train rides to road games took days, with teammates marking time by telling stories, playing cards, passing a bottle of booze, then passing out. Like any family, especially one with a mostly Irish temperament, there were plenty of internal disputes. Burkett, for one, was known for his quicksilver temper. On one road trip to Chicago, Tebeau found himself explaining away a black eye to the press as the result of a misunderstanding with his center fielder. On the Baltimore team, John McGraw was equally as well known for his battles with teammates, even a well-publicized one with the easygoing Willie Keeler. But once teams took the field, any internal animosity was redirected toward the opponent, toward the opposing team's fans, even toward the cities where they played.

Though Sockalexis played the appropriate role of reticent rookie among his teammates, his antics in Cleveland's saloons were documented from his arrival. A mention in a *Sporting Life* column was the first indication of the rookie's love of the nightlife: "Sockalexis, the Indian, makes friends fast. He already knows half the sports in town, and he's only been here three days." With the team, however, acceptance was based solely on talent and production. Judging from the early returns, Sockalexis was well on his way to membership.

While Frank Robison was in New York, Tebeau was fiddling with his lineup. But as the manager tried to build a better team, he had an uneasy feeling. There was more than the usual pressure on him during the 1897 season. He knew better than anyone that if Cleveland finished out of the pennant, his and the team's future were uncertain. Tebeau was dealing with a unpredictable owner, a fickle fan base, and several question marks on the field. What exacerbated the situation was a nationwide recession that threatened the stability of the whole National League.

Undoubtedly, financial pressure fueled Robison's war on the clergy for his right to play Sunday ball. But it also filtered directly down to Tebeau and, by extension, to an unwitting Sockalexis. The rookie had a plate filled with pressures of his own. The day the Potawatomi Indians came to watch him play in Michigan was perhaps his first indication that he was a representative of a bigger issue than just baseball. Back on Indian Island, newspaper accounts of his accomplishments on the ball field were read with proud fervor. Even his father, whose dislike of his son's ambition spawned the fantastic story of his oceangoing canoe trip, had become a believer and a fan. But any positive power gained from those who rooted for him was greatly overshadowed by the sea of negativity in which he had to perform. Though somewhat mollified with the ending of the Indian wars, the white man's perception of American Indians ranged from a sideshow attraction to lingering deep-seated resentment. Rarely did white America consider them equal.

In the written histories of Sockalexis there are few mentions of how he handled the oppression. In the account of the fight at Popcorn Jenny's there is the inference that a racial slur (along with too much alcohol) prompted Sockalexis to his rage. In a rare interview in the *Cleveland Plain Dealer*, Sockalexis talked about how he handled abuse from fans and opposing players: "No matter where we play I go through the same ordeal, and at the present time I am so used to it that at times I forget to smile at my tormentors." Sockalexis went on to say that he thought the abuse just "part of the game." Some fifty years later, a twenty-seven-year-old Dodger rookie would go through something similar. Jackie Robinson, too, was constantly showered with epithets from irate fans and opposing players. Both players endured a national press that labeled them by their race; Robinson was often called "Bojangles of the base paths." Both arrived in the major leagues on the heels of illustrious college careers. Both were enormous drawing cards. But there were also big differences with the two players' experiences.

Robinson was well aware of his place in history. Branch Rickey's "noble experiment," as the press tagged it, would draw tremendous attention to both the Dodger owner and his star player. Robinson's rookie season was a cement block in a foundation that would become the civil rights movement. Though in the minority, there was a loud and powerful lobby among celebrities and the press championing the integration of major leagues. By 1947, Robinson's rookie year, black soldiers had fought and died on the battlefields of Italy and France. Patriotic fever swelled when Joe Louis defeated Max Schmelling, and when Jesse Owens ran past the Germans in the Munich Olympics. Robinson was also a plug to a huge pool of talent in the Negro leagues. Once that talent began to seek its proper level, the major leagues became a far better game. Ultimately, Jackie Robinson represented a race that could no longer be denied by white America.

In Sockalexis's time, government troops had already crushed the Indian nation. The voice then for reform in relations between Native Americans and whites was small and often horribly misguided. Children were forcibly taken from reservations and placed in government schools to "Americanize" them. The Carlisle Indian School, which would go on to produce athletes like Jim Thorpe and Charles Albert "Chief" Bender, were run under the edict of "Kill the Indian, save the child." There were no sports heroes that blazed the trail for Sockalexis; the only Indian heroes in popular culture then were romanticized warriors from decades past. The encroachment of white settlers and the Indian wars had significantly diminished the Native population. Those who remained were herded onto reservations where they could not participate in the white experience, which led to extreme ignorance on both sides. In the eyes of white America, Sockalexis represented more of a myth than a race.

But in that spring of 1897, Sockalexis was protected by a kind of rookie innocence. The only thing that mattered to him was playing baseball. He believed he could do anything he wanted between the foul lines and no power on earth could stop him. And for one standout summer, much like Jackie Robinson after him, he did just that.

With a massive influx of immigrants throughout the second half of the nineteenth century, ethnic neighborhoods in Cleveland grew at an astounding rate. Though the city's industrial base offered employment to many, the depression of the mid-1890s spawned poverty and slums. One of the first of these impoverished neighborhoods was the Haymarket, located in what is now downtown Cleveland. Saloons lined the streets of that neighborhood, numbering as many as thirty by the turn of the century. Public drunkenness was commonplace. Beer, sold in two-quart tin buckets, cost just a nickel. The Young Women's Christian Association offered lodging for drunks at the Friendly Inn. Whiskey Island was another downtrodden section ripe with alcohol abuse. A triangle of land that jutted out into the Cuyahoga River, the "island" was an overwhelmingly Irish settlement. The name came from a distillery built there in the 1830s. Along with the distillery, iron works and docks operated on the Cuyahoga. Only one mile long and a third of a mile at it widest, with twenty-two streets dissecting it, the neighborhood supported more than a dozen saloons.

As alcohol abuse in Cleveland swelled, so did the temperance movement. Former boxing champ John L. Sullivan, who once displayed with pride his penchant for inebriation, lent his name to the temperance cause. Cleveland was the birthplace of the Women's Christian Temperance Union, founded in 1874. By 1897 its ranks nationwide had swelled to a quarter million. Women marched en masse into saloons and fell on their knees to pray. The WCTU was backed by the full weight of the Protestant ministers of Cleveland. Sermons about the evils of Sunday baseball were alternated, or combined, with ones on the evils of alcohol.

In one sermon early in March of 1897, the Reverend B. G. Newton of the Franklin Avenue Congregational Church called professional baseball players in general, and the Indians in particular, "tramps" who should be put in a penitentiary. "They are enemies to thrift, honesty and industry," the reverend said. "The saloon-keeper does not have a greater influence for evil than a professional ball player." Society women of Cleveland were convinced. "I don't believe in condoning one evil and attacking another. Baseball on Sunday will hasten the opening of saloons on Sunday. It is an opening wedge," said one churchgoing lady in the *Cleveland Plain Dealer*. "It will do such an injury to very young men and boys by attracting them there among a motley throng of drunken and vicious characters and thus eradicating all thoughts of the Sabbath from their minds. It will be no credit to our beautiful city to have Sunday baseball," said another.

By 1893 the temperance movement had expanded into the political arena. The Ohio Anti-Saloon League, founded that year, was made up of influential members of church and community. They raised great sums of money and lobbied lawmakers to enact bills enforcing prohibition. By 1897 their monthly newsletter had a subscription of twenty-five thousand. "The saloon must go!" was their rallying cry.

In response, the Ohio State Liquor League of saloonkeepers raised considerable funds of their own, publishing weekly trade papers extolling the rights of free enterprise and free choice. In a publicity war, liquor men took out ads in newspapers thinly disguised as news stories. One, in the *Plain Dealer*, quoted a Presbyterian minister named Mills: "I have used Duffy's Pure Malt Whiskey with great benefit to my wife, who is a confirmed invalid. . . . I am not afraid to recommend Duffy's Malt Whiskey as the purest and most efficient preparation as a medicine that I know of, and my experience is a large one."

Despite the growing influence of the temperance movement, immigrants held fast to their right to drink. Saloons opened on Sunday in direct defiance. The same hardscrabble men who thought it their God-given right to drink on Sunday were the ones who rode Frank Robison's streetcars to League Park.

In 1885, *Plain Dealer* publisher Liberty Emery Holden built the Hollenden Hotel in a downtown section of Cleveland. At the rear of the hotel, on Vincent Avenue, a street only one block in length, taverns and restaurants opened to accommodate Hollenden guests. Unlike the bawdy saloons of the Haymarket and Whiskey Island, Short Vincent, as it became known, drew a somewhat better class of patrons. Barbershop quartets sang and Scott Joplin's rags filled the night air. The saloons were filled with dandies—male peacocks dressed to the nines in straw-brimmed hats called "boaters" and starched collars.

By the 1890s, however, Short Vincent began to fray at the edges. The bicycle might have been all the rage on Euclid Avenue, where women riders began to pull up their Victorian skirts to show a bit of ankle, but on Short Vincent more than just ankles were shown.

According to one researcher, Sockalexis began drinking alcohol as far back as his days at Holy Cross, where coaches posted players at the corners of his bed to "keep him from searching the night for liquor." His drinking was a certainty at Notre Dame. But nothing he had experienced could compare to the temptation of the Cleveland night. Sockalexis was young and good looking. Before he even played his first National League game, the press had made him a star. In a town and a time where many struggled for food and to pay rent, his money was as long as train smoke. The bawdy Cleveland saloons brimmed with sharpies and hangers-on. Some of the women were as easy as a soft fly ball. The trap was oiled and stretched, and the Indian, dressed in English tweed with a child's smile on his face, was just about to stroll into it.

SOCKALEXIS' DAY.

The Indian Covers Himself With All Kinds of Glory.

And There Are Other Indians.

The Colts Make a Good Race and a Splendid Game is the Result—The L. A. W. Rupture Will Mean War to the Knife — Central Armory Match Races—Running Results—Other Sporting.

The Standing.

Clubs.	W.	L.	Pr.Ct.
Baltimore	10	2	833
Louisville	7	3	700
Pittsburg	7	3	700
Cincinnati	7	4	636
Philadelphia	8	5	615
Cleveland	6	6	500
New York	5	5	500
Boston	5	6	455
Brooklyn	4	8	333
St. Louis	3	8	273
Chicago	3	9	250
Washington	2	8	200

Today's Games.

Chicago at Cleveland.
Cincinnati at Pittsburg.
St. Louis at Louisville.
Baltimore at Philadelphia.
Brooklyn at New York.
Washington at Boston.

Cleveland 6—Chicago 5.

The man who said that there are no good Indians except dead Indians, or words to that effect, surely never saw Louis Sockalexis, late of the Penobscot tribe, but now of the tribe of Tebeau. Sockalexis is certainly not a "dead one" and as to his being good! The word does not express his quality. The baseball fans who witnessed Sock's performance yesterday will agree that he is the best Indian that ever wandered down the pike. Pocahontas is never a marker to him and all the other good Indians of history fade into insignificance before the new found hero. There was a battle out at League park yesterday and to Sockalexis the glory of the day and the victory is due. He not only won the battle by his war club, with which he pounded out three singles and a three-bagger, but (losing the simile) he

fly to Lange scored Tebeau, but McKean quit easily.

Pfeffer's single was all that went Chicago's way in the eighth, but Sockalexis began Cleveland's half with a three-bagger to left. Dahlen got O'Connor's fly, but Blake's liner was too hot for him. Socks scored, but Blake and Zimmer were doubled up.

Even in the last inning, after two men were out, Chicago come very close to tying the score, for Dahlen hit to left for two bases. Lange and Thornton followed with singles and these hits, together with a wild pitch, scored two runs. Burkett ended the game by taking Ryan's long fly from close against the fence. Score:

Cleveland.	A.B.	R.	H.	O.	A.	E.
Burkett, l. f.	3	1	1	2	0	0
McKean, s. s.	5	0	0	0	5	0
Sockalexis, r. f.	4	2	4	5	0	0
O'Connor, 1b	5	1	1	16	0	1
Blake, r. f.	5	0	3	2	0	0
Zimmer, c.	5	0	1	0	1	0
Tebeau, 2b	3	2	1	0	3	0
Wallace, 3b	3	0	2	2	2	0
Young, p.	3	0	2	0	7	0
Totals	36	6	15	27	18	1

Chicago.	A.B.	R.	H.	O.	A.	E.
Everitt, 3b	1	0	0	0	0	0
McCormick, 3b	4	0	3	0	2	0
Dahlen, s. s.	4	2	3	4	2	1
Lange, c. f.	4	1	2	4	0	2
Thornton, l. f.	5	1	2	0	1	0
Ryan, r. f.	5	0	0	2	0	0
Decker, 1b	4	1	1	7	1	0
Pfeffer, 2b	4	0	1	3	4	0
Kittridge, c.	4	0	1	4	0	0
Denzer, p.	4	0	1	0	1	0
Totals	39	5	14	24	11	3

Cleveland ..... 3 0 1 0 0 0 1 1 *—6
Chicago .... 1 0 0 2 0 0 0 0 2—5

Earned runs—Cleveland 3, Chicago 2. Two-base hits—Denzer, Dahlen. Three-base hit—Sockalexis. Home run—Dahlen. Sacrifice hits—Wallace, Lange. Stolen bases—Sockalexis 2, Young 2, Burkett, Blake, McCormick, Thornton, Lange. Double plays—McCormick, Pfeffer, to Decker; Dahlen to Pfeffer. First base on balls—By Denzer 5, (Burkett 2, Sockalexis, Tebeau, Young). Left on bases—Cleveland 12, Chicago 8. Struck out—By Denzer, McKean. Passed balls—Zimmer 1. Wild pitch—Young. Time—2:00. Umpire—McDonald.

A Few Features.

There is no longer a doubt that Bobby Wallace will be a fixture at third. His work already eclipses McGarr, and besides that Bobby is just learning. Two of his assists yesterday were on the phenomenal order and he is batting pretty well, too. McGarr will be retained as a utility man, but unless more accidents occur to the infield he will not be seen in a game for some time to come.

Blake is hitting the ball right along and playing his field in a manner that would insure his being retained even if there were a half a dozen pair of Socks on the team instead of half a pair. McAleer has not been missed so far and neither has Childs, thanks to Blake and Tebeau.

It is a remarkable score that makes McKean out the only man on the team without a hit. Four times yesterday did the big short stop pound the ball hard but unlucky, for somebody just managed to get to it in time to make trouble.

Three singles and a three-bagger, a total

Earned runs—Pittsburg Two-base hit—Irwin. 2, Lyons, Sugden. Ho sacrifice hits—Burk, McF enstein. Stolen bases Burk, Peitz. First ba len 2, off Breitenstein Smith. First base on Killen 1. Struck ou Breitenstein 3. Left 11, Cincinnati 6. Time—2:15.

Baltimore 13—P

PHILADELPHIA, M Philadelphia had an game today and Baltin The hitting was chiefl had been given to r pitching on both sides bases being given on batting of Cooley w feature. Fifield pitc innings for Philadelph lieved by Wheeler Score:

Philadelphia.	A
Cooley, c. f.	
Geier, r. f.	
Lajoie, 1b	
Delehanty, l. f.	
Boyle, c.	
Cross, 3b	
Hallman, 2b	
Gillen, s. s.	
Fifield, p.	
Wheeler, p.	
Totals	

Baltimore.	A
Keeler, r. f.	
Jennings, s. s.	
Kelley, l. f.	
Doyle, 1b	
Stenzel, c. f.	
Quinn, 3b	
Reitz, 2b	
Robinson, c.	
Corbett, p.	
Totals	

Philadelphia ......
Baltimore ......

Earned runs—Phila 6. Two-base hits—Co man, Fifield, Quinn, Jennings, Kelley, Doy Jennings, Reitz, Doy Doyle. First base on off Wheeler 3, off pitcher—Boyle 2, Gille Struck out—By Whee Wild pitches—Wheeler on bases—Philadelph Time—2:45. Umpire

Boston 4—W

BOSTON, May 7 whitewashed by Bosto good game. Errors w ting was not particul fielding was sharp. five men to one for t Collins' work at the Attendance 2,200. Scc

Boston.	A
Hamilton, c. f.	
Tenney, 1b	
Long, s. s.	
Duffy, l. f.	
Yeager, r. f.	
Lowe, 2b	

5

LATE SPRING 1897—*The Free Thought Lyceum supports Sunday baseball as long as other Cleveland businesses are also allowed to operate on the Sabbath. In a scathing pronouncement, the city's intellectuals call the Protestant churches "tax dodgers." Following the lead of William Randolph Hearst and Joseph Pulitzer, Liberty E. Holden's* Cleveland Plain Dealer *begins to beat the drums for war with Spain in Cuba. "Six Little Tailors," a haberdashery on Superior Street, charges $12.50 for an "honest" suit or overcoat made to order. The* Plain Dealer *reports that a priest has invented a bulletproof vest in Chicago; in a test, eight bullets from a .30 caliber Winchester rifle were fired at the cloth and "failed to drive the foremost bullet more than a third of the way through the fabric." Trolley fares in Cleveland are raised from one to two cents but include "excursions."*

* * * *

BY THE TIME THE CLEVELAND NINE rolled into Cincinnati for the second series of the season, Sockalexis was already big news around the country. A writer for the *Sporting News* characterized him as a "drawing card" for the Cleveland team and an asset to the whole league. The *Plain Dealer* sportswriters, too, had dropped the moniker "Spiders" from their lexicon altogether and had begun to call the team "the Indians" exclusively. For the rhymers and the wordplayers of the day, the Indian's presence was a bonanza. The team was "Tebeau's Tribe" or "Warriors" who "scalped" their opponents. Tebeau himself became "Medicine Man." Sockalexis was labeled "Chief Sock-it-to-'em," or "Sock-it-on-the-nose," and "Chief Not-afraid-of-his-job." The *Plain Dealer* ran cartoons of the Indian adorned in headdress, brandishing a tomahawk. In what was the practice of the day, sportswriters and others composed lengthy poems about baseball and its heroes. Sockalexis inspired quite a few. This one was written after a home run he hit against St. Louis:

> *As the Browns stood mute and spellbound*
> *In their flood bedraggled ball field,*
> *On the banks of the Mississippi,*
> *Up spoke mighty Patsy Tebeau,*
> *"Henceforth he shall be our right field,*
> *Somewhere else will play Young Blakie*
> *'Ansome' Arry is a good one,*
> *But he surely is not in it*
> *When it comes to clearing bases,*
> *When it comes to swiping home runs,*
> *And hereafter and forever,*
> *Sox shall hold supreme dominion*

'Till he shows a streak of yellow,
'Till his batting eye deserts him
He's the stuff and he's the people . . ."

Obscured by all the hype surrounding their star player was the fact that the team was winless after the first four games of the season. Only a bottom-of-the-ninth circus catch by Sockalexis kept them from falling to 0–5. Poor pitching was the primary reason for Cleveland's woes. John Pappalau was rocked in his first outing against Louisville. By the second week of the season, sportswriters were already predicting a quick end to the highly touted rookie pitcher's major league career. Cy Young, too, was not his usual unhittable self. In the first game of the season he had slid badly into second base and twisted his ankle. He couldn't push off the mound with any power, and his whirlwind fastball became just ordinary.

The first two losses of the season had come against Louisville, one of the weakest teams in the league. The Indians then limped into Cincinnati to face a team that had won its first four games. In the opening game of the series it looked like Cleveland's fortunes were about to turn around. The day was dry and sunny, but a stiff wind blew in from center field. Crab Burkett led off the game with a lined single to left. Cupid Childs, the next batter up, smacked a shot that looked as though it would easily clear the field of play. At the crack of the bat, Eddie Burke, the Cincinnati outfielder, turned and streaked toward the deepest recesses in left. When he turned back to find the ball, the wind had held it up. Burke reversed direction and dove in a gallant try, but the ball was jarred from his mitt as he hit the ground.

With runners on second and third, war whoops from the five thousand or so fans taunted the next batter as he walked to the plate. On the mound for the Reds was Billy Rhines, a veteran who still threw in the underhand, submarine style of pitching from baseball's infancy. With the Reds infielders called in for a play at the plate, Sockalexis slapped an underhand fastball over the second baseman's head, driving in both Burkett and Childs. Boos and whoops cascaded from the stands as the Indian stood on first base.

The war whoops turned to solid cheers in the fifth, when the Indian made a spectacular diving catch in the outfield. Despite the team's third straight loss, the Cleveland papers hailed Sock as a "star of the first order." The following day, the star tumbled to earth.

Sockalexis was overmatched against Cincinnati's southpaw, Teddy Breitenstein. The same sportswriters who had exalted Sock the day before now wondered whether he could hit left-handed pitching. Against Breitenstein, he struck out ugly three times. But it wasn't the left-handed delivery he was struggling with. Even in those early years of baseball, word of a hitter's weakness traveled quickly throughout the league. One Cincinnati pitcher confided to a sportswriter that Sockalexis couldn't hit the drop pitch (curveball). Breitenstein had fed the Indian a steady diet of them.

In the next series, against the St. Louis Browns, Sockalexis still looked clueless at the plate, going one for five, the one hit being an infield dribbler. In his defense, the weather had turned bitter, with a raw wet wind blowing across the field. Though the Indian seemed uncomfortable at the plate, in the field he was nothing short of spectacular. Cleveland led for most of the game and was up 6–3 in the sixth frame on the strength of a long home run by shortstop Ed McKean.

But as the dank day turned nearly dark, St. Louis scratched back. After pushing two runs across the plate in the ninth, the Browns had tied the score, 6–6. With the winning run on third, Browns catcher Ed McFarland hit a long drive to right. With his back turned toward the infield, and running at full gallop, the Indian seemed to disappear into the darkness. The umpire wasn't sure if the catch had been made—until the Indian's stride slowed to a trot and he held up the ball. In the bleachers and on the benches there was something of a stunned silence.

Because of the darkness, the umpire called the game. Perhaps looking to light a fire under his team, Tebeau took exception to the ruling. Not that Patsy needed a reason to start a row with an ump; he didn't get along with any umpire, and he especially despised the ump that day, a fellow named McDonald. Tebeau accused McDonald of being a "homer"—prone to call close plays in favor of the home team. Tebeau wasn't necessarily delusional. Considering the physical abuse umps then were subject to, being a homer wasn't a bad tactic to reduce bodily harm.

In the ever-growing darkness, Tebeau and McDonald stood chin-to-chin. The St. Louis cranks, of course, loved it. For two bits they saw a game and a fight too. Fueled by the crowd noise, Patsy grabbed McDonald by the throat. Several Cleveland players had to pull their manager off the umpire. When things finally settled down, the game was officially over and the park emptied.

After the game, at a downtown St. Louis hotel, the manager along with his players sidled up to the bar. Just when the stories were getting good, McDonald burst into the barroom. A *Plain Dealer* sportswriter witnessed the confrontation: "Pat could not see what the use of fighting off the field was, and would not make it a go." The tension in the barroom was broken when Tebeau offered to buy a beer. The manager's gesture of détente was accepted, and the two adversaries wound up with arms draped over each other's shoulders. Both knew, however, that their new friendship would last only until the next disputed call.

The next afternoon, the Indians seemed like a different team. In the first inning, McKean doubled, Sock hit a sac fly, Childs drew a base on balls, and both he and McKean scored on Jimmy "Loafer" McAleer's single to left. Unlike Cleveland's pitching to date, Zeke Wilson was solid on the mound, allowing no hits through the first four innings. Wilson had played his first full season for Cleveland the year before, going 16–11 and solidifying himself as the third starter, behind Nig Cuppy and Cy Young. With two outs in the fifth inning, Cleveland scored twice more. Sock began the rally with a sharp single to center. Tebeau, who contributed to the team as both manager and player, then hit a dribbler to short. The throw went over the first baseman's mitt and, in an awesome display of speed, Sockalexis circled the bases and scored. But it was in the eighth inning when Sock brought the St. Louis fans to their feet. The day before, McKean had hit a home run that landed in Chute Lake well beyond the right field fence. According to sportswriters, it was the longest home run ever hit at Sportsman's Park. The Indian was about to rewrite history.

With two outs in the frame and McKean on first, courtesy of a base on balls, Sockalexis came to the plate. As usual, throughout the game the local cranks had showered him with the most derisive of cheers. That week, *Sporting Life* reported that the "derisive Ki Yis" from the stands didn't seem to bother him. There are such players gifted with this inner peace while performing at their peak—being in the zone, as it's called—that allows them to witness their surroundings as if they were happening in slow motion, like Ken Griffey Jr. does in today's Pepsi commercial. Boos and curses are filtered and heard as nothing more than the inane chatter of a monkey house. More times than not under such conditions, Sockalexis's face softened with a polite smile. And more times than not, the smile would eventually win over even the vilest of crowds.

The sound was not like today's crisp crack of a well-struck baseball; it was more like a thud, like a slab of prime rib slapped on a butcher's block. The yarn in the balls then was hand rolled; the raised stitching that knitted together the cowhide made Frankenstein look like an "after" picture in the office of a Beverly Hills plastic surgeon. In the stands, heads snapped to follow the majestic arc ever higher into the pale blue sky. There was never a question that the ball was a home run, only how far it would travel. McKean's record homer of the day before lasted as long as it took Sockalexis's ball to splash.

Sock's problems with the curveball didn't last long. On May 1, against St. Louis, he was four for five, including two triples, one that drove in three runs and broke the game open. Cleveland was playing terrific ball, and the Indian was the reason. He seemed to have sparked something in his fellow players. In the field, Burkett made a Sock-like catch to snuff out a rally. At the plate, the Cleveland nine racked up ten hits against the Browns' starter, Red Donahue. Sportswriters caught Indian fever: "[Cleveland] jammed the ball around the lot with reckless abandon and playful ferocity that usually characterizes a tribe of Indians doing a scalp dance upon an expiring foe."

Truly, the Indian swung the war club in the ninth. St. Louis had wriggled out of several situations that would have put the game out of reach. In the last inning, with the score 2–1 in Cleveland's favor, the Indians loaded the bases on two errors and a base on balls. Sockalexis swung at the first pitch and smashed it over the center fielder's head; three scored and the victory was secured. With the season just a couple of weeks old, the Indian was steering the team's destiny. Every day now, it seemed, Sockalexis's play in the field or at the plate was determining the outcome of the game.

On May 2, while still in New York, Frank Robison received a telegram from his team's manager. Tebeau was wiring his boss to extol the Indian's performance. In turn, Robison told reporters how happy he was with the rookie's play. "Today I consider Sockalexis the greatest find of the year," Robison said. "His work has been better 100 per cent than I thought he would ever play." Although Doc Powers, the Holy Cross captain, was the guiding force behind Sock's assent to the majors and so much of his early success, others began to take credit for discovering the phenom. Crab Burkett told sportswriters that he had watched the Indian's career unfold at Holy Cross and had wired Tebeau about him. "He is a wonder," Burkett wrote in the wire, "but I can't spell his name. Just send on a blank contract and I will try to sign him." But in New York, Robison said that John Montgomery Ward was responsible for bringing Sockalexis to his attention.

Ward had a Hall of Fame career as a pitcher, infielder, outfielder, and later manager. After developing arm trouble early in his career, he taught himself to throw left-handed and moved to the outfield. But perhaps even more impressive was that Ward had managed to obtain a degree in political science from Columbia University, graduating with honors while playing professional baseball. Throughout his schooling and career, Ward strongly believed that the financial balance in baseball was unfairly tipped in the owners' favor. In 1885 he helped organize the Brotherhood of Professional Baseball Players, the first players' union. In 1890 he helped form the Player's League. With promises of better salaries and the abolition of baseball's reserve clause, which gave owners total power over a player's destiny, nearly one half of the established players of the National League defected.

Though at first it looked like Ward's league would be a success—in 1890 the Player's League drew more fans than the National League—without major financial backing the Player's League folded after just one season. Ward's rebellion cast him as a troublemaker in the eyes of major league management. But his pure baseball talent won him a place back in the National League in 1891 with the Brooklyn Bridegrooms. After he retired in 1894, Ward earned his law degree from Columbia and practiced law full time. Many of his clients were friends and teammates from his baseball days. He represented a star pitcher in a highly publicized contractual dispute with New York Giants owner Andrew Freedman.

Ward first saw Sockalexis play at Holy Cross. In an era of unspeakable racism, Ward judged ballplayers not on the color of their skin but purely on talent. In 1885 he urged Giants owner, John Day, to sign a black pitcher by the name of George Stovey. Almost to a player, the Giants told Day they would not play with a black. Though Stovey was indeed a talent who could help the team, Day wouldn't take a chance of player insurrection, and he didn't sign the pitcher.

Two years later, in 1887, Stovey would be involved in a controversy that would mark the beginning of major league baseball's unwritten policy to exclude blacks and other minorities from the game. Cap Anson, the manager of the Chicago franchise of the National League, refused to let his team play in an exhibition game against Newark's International League team that fielded Stovey and other blacks. An avowed racist, Anson was the most vocal proponent of exclusionism. So powerful was Anson's voice that not only did the National League follow his mandate but the International League soon adopted the same policy. While Sockalexis was smacking baseballs and mahogany bars at Holy Cross, a kind soul was gently guiding his destiny.

In early 1897, on one of the newfangled telephones that then numbered in the hundreds of thousands in America, Ward placed a call to Robison. It's doubtful that Robison thought about his place in history when he signed Sockalexis. More likely he was thinking of dollars. He expected the Indian's presence to spin the turnstiles at League Park. But Robison was one tough character. With the owners meeting in New York as his stage, in the midst of peers who kowtowed to the Ansons of the league, he announced his pleasure with a red man's performance—and thanked equalitarian John Ward for bringing the Indian to his attention. His actions were no less courageous than Branch Rickey's fifty years later.

With the season just a few weeks old, Sockalexis had gained more than just Robison's admiration and acceptance. The team too had opened its notoriously closed ranks and welcomed the rookie. The Indian was just easy to like. Scribes of the day wrote often of Sockalexis's easygoing nature and sense of humor. Jack "Peach Pie" O'Connor was the team joker, and Sockalexis assumed the role of sidekick. "No member of the Cleveland team can see the point to a joke or a pun quicker than Sock," remarked the *Plain Dealer*. Burkett, too, had a close relationship with the Indian. In the well-worn saying, the veteran took the rookie under his wing. On the Cleveland team, Burkett continued the coach/father role he'd had with Sockalexis at Holy Cross. Often Burkett would be seen giving batting tips and fielding pointers. The Crab even lent the Indian his gamer (favorite bat). But despite all the warm feelings the Indian generated, the real reason the team accepted him was that they were much better with him in right field.

On May 6 the Indians had a chance to move to .500 with a win against Cincinnati. The Reds jumped out to a 2–0 lead in the top of the second, but Cleveland came back in their half and tied it on a homer by Sockalexis that cleared the right field fence and landed on Lexington Avenue. On the surface the war whoops and tomahawk chops in the stands had the same biting derisiveness as they did on the road. But the fans here, at League Park, had opened their hearts to him—at least as a baseball player. As was the case on those first long train rides with his teammates, where acceptance was gained by productivity on the diamond, so too was approval by cranks. But this Greek chorus was fickle, and racial difference was an easy target should the drama turn bad.

In Cincinnati's half of the third, the Reds threatened to retake the lead. With runners on first and third and one out, shortstop Claude Ritchey hit a blistering line drive to deep right. With the ball almost by him, Sock dove and held on as his prone body slammed the outfield grass. The Reds runner, Charlie Irvin, tagged third and streaked toward home. In one graceful motion, the Indian tumbled to his feet and came up throwing. The ball hit Chief Zimmer's glove before Irvin began to slide. If thrown from the mound instead of right field, the ball would have been a called strike. If there had been a hitter in the box and he foolishly tried to swing at it, it would have been a strike. "The play was a remarkable one," wrote one sportswriter, "and will not soon be forgotten."

With Cincinnati leading 3–2 in the bottom of the seventh, the Indians mounted a rally. Sockalexis singled to center and O'Connor walked, putting men at first and second. With only one out, Harry Blake came to the plate. He took the first three pitches for balls, and when Bill "Wee Willie" Damman, the Reds hurler, let the fourth pitch fly, it hit Blake squarely on the back. Instead of awarding him first to load the bases, the umpire—McDonald again—ruled that there was no pitch, or rather that there was no rule that covered such a pitch. Though for the most part players treated umpires unfairly, there was a patent ineptitude among the boys in blue.

In 1887 baseball had adopted the rule awarding first base to a hit batter. (Perhaps McDonald was too busy giving arm signals and forgot about the rulebook; Cincinnati's outfielder Dummy Hoy, who was deaf, had asked baseball to direct umps to signal balls and strikes so he would know the count, and baseball complied.) With the recent altercation still fresh in both parties' minds, it was only a matter of time before Tebeau and McDonald went at it again.

The simmering situation worsened as Blake, instead of standing on first base, popped out to the infield. When Zimmer followed with a long fly to center that would have sacrificed the Indian easily from third and tied the score, Tebeau was on the verge of exploding. He would have, too, if not for the fact that he followed Zimmer in the batting order. With Sockalexis dancing off second, Tebeau hit a sharp grounder just to the right of the third baseman. This time the Indian's speed worked against him. The ball clipped the rookie's spike, and Tebeau was called out by interference. The final was 3–2, in favor of Cincinnati. The Indian along with several other Cleveland players escorted their fuming manager from the field.

Though the loss stung, there was a bigger picture to consider. The Indians were playing as a team, and Sockalexis was truly a part of it. The season was getting interesting, and the Indians had the hopes of Cleveland's cranks flying.

Sockalexis Does Some Great Work.

He Makes a Decided Hit With the Fans and Three of Them for the Team—More Talk of the Players' Organization—Three Tie Games— John L. Sullivan in Town and in Earnest—Other Sporting.

YESTERDAY'S RESULTS.

Cincinnati ..... 6—Cleveland 3
Brooklyn ...... 4—Baltimore 3
Louisville ..... 3—Pittsburg 3
New York ..... 3—Washington .. 3
Chicago .... 9—St. Louis 2
Philadelphia .. 8—Boston 8

The Standing.

Clubs.	W.	L.	Pr.Ct.
Cincinnati	4	0	1000
Philadelphia	4	0	1000
Louisville	2	0	1000
Baltimore	3	1	750
Brooklyn	3	1	750
Pittsburg	1	1	500
St. Louis	1	2	333
Washington	1	3	250
Chicago	1	3	250
Cleveland	0	3	000
New York	0	3	000
Boston	0	4	000

Today's Games.

Cleveland at Cincinnati.
Pittsburg at Louisville.
Chicago at St. Louis.
Brooklyn at Baltimore.
Washington at New York.
Boston at Philadelphia.

Cincinnati 6—Cleveland 3.

Special to the Plain Dealer.

CINCINNATI, April 26.—Patsy Tebeau's Indians did not stumble across their batting eye en route from Louisville, and that explains their defeat at the hands of Ewing's warriors here today. After Patsy lost those two scalps at Louisville he consoled himself by hoping for better luck at Ewingville, but Dame Fortune did not meet him at the depot, nor was she within hearing distance of Patsy's pleas after he arrived at league park. From a local standpoint of view it was a beautiful contest. Two of the three errors made in the game resulted in runs, but on a whole the fielding was strong on both sides.

The bright particular star of the game was Warrior Louis Sockalexis. He was naturally the center of attraction after the visitors reached the grounds. He was greeted with war whoops and Indian yells, but as the game progressed and Socks began to hit and field, he was given an ovation. The Indian is a star, at least that is the impression that the 4,420 fans drew from his work today. Every one of his three fielding chances were of the most difficult order, and though it was the first time in his career that he had ever played

Cincinnati ... . 0 2 0 0 1 1 0 2 *—6
Cleveland .... 2 0 0 0 0 1 0 0 —3

Earned runs—Cincinnati 2. Two-base hits—Sockalexis, McPhee. Three-base hits—Ritchey, Rhines. Stolen bases—Burke, Irwin, Ritchey, McPhee, McAleer, Hoy, O'Connor. Double play—Childs and Tebeau. First base on balls—Off Rhines 1, off Wilson 1. Left on bases—Cleveland 3. Struck out—By Rhines 3. Passed ball—O'Connor. Wild pitch—Rhines. Time—1.45. Umpire—Sheridan.

Chicago 9—St. Louis 2.

ST. LOUIS, April 26.—The Colts won the first game of the season with the Browns today. Hutchison pitched against his old companions and was hit hard until he retired in the seventh inning, being replaced by Kissinger, who held the visitors down to two hits, neither of which was scored. The weather was perfect. Attendance 1,000. Score:

St. Louis.	A.B.	R.	H.	O.	A.	E.
Douglas, l. f.	3	0	1	0	0	0
Dowd, c. f.	5	0	4	3	0	0
Turner, r. f.	5	0	1	4	0	0
Connor, 1b	4	0	0	12	0	0
Hartman, 3b	4	0	2	2	2	1
Bierbauer, 2b	4	0	1	2	2	0
Cross, s. s.	4	0	0	1	7	0
Murphy, c.	4	1	1	3	2	1
Hutchison, p.	3	1	1	0	1	0
Kissinger, p.	1	0	0	0	2	0
Totals	37	2	11	27	16	2

Chicago.	A.B.	R.	H.	O.	A.	E.
Everitt, 3b	6	1	1	1	4	0
Dahlen, s. s.	3	2	1	2	2	0
Lange, c. f.	6	3	2	2	0	0
Thornton, l. f.	6	0	4	2	0	1
Ryan, r. f.	4	1	1	3	0	0
Decker, 1b	5	1	4	11	2	0
Pfeffer, 2b	4	1	2	0	2	1
Callahan, p.	5	1	2	1	2	0
Anson, c.	3	0	0	5	0	0
Totals	42	9	17	27	12	2

Chicago ...... 0 2 1 2 1 0 2 0 1—9
St. Louis ..... 0 0 1 0 1 0 0 0 0—2

Earned runs—Chicago 5. Two-base hits—Hartman, Thornton, Ryan. Three-base hit—Pfeffer. Stolen bases—Bierbauer, Everitt, Dahlen 2, Lange. Double play—Callahan, Decker and Anson. First base on balls—Off Callahan 3, off Hutchison 7. Struck out—By Callahan 3, by Hutchison 1. Time—2:20. Umpire—McDonald.

New York 3—Washington 3.

NEW YORK, April 26.—The regular baseball season was opened in this city today when the Senators, suffering from successive defeats, met the New Yorks, who lost the first three games at Philadelphia last week. At the end of the ninth inning the score was tied, and the visitors had just started to play the first half of the tenth when a windstorm arose. The game was called with the score tied. Score:

New York.	A.B.	R.	H.	O.	A.	E.
Van Haltren, c. f.	4	1	4	3	0	1
Tiernan, r. f.	4	1	1	0	0	0
Gleason, 2b	5	0	0	5	5	1
Joyce, 3b	2	0	1	2	4	1
Davis, s. s.	4	0	1	1	0	2
Beckley, 1b	3	0	0	12	1	1
Gettig, l. f.	4	0	0	1	0	0
Warner, c.	3	1	1	3	1	0
Doheny, p.	4	0	2	0	6	0
Totals	33	3	10	27	17	6

Washington.	A.B.	R.	H.	O.	A.	E.
Abbey, r. f.	1	0	0	0	0	0
Demont, s. s.	4	0	3	3	3	0

Earned runs—Lo
First base by error
burg 2. First base
off Tannehill 2. Le
3, Pittsburg 12. St
by Tannehill 5.
Lyons. Three-base
Two-base hit—Ely.
ing. Stolen bases—
die, Donovan, Sugde
play—Padden, Lyon
Brodie. Time—2:35.

Philadelphi

PHILADELPHIA, .
Philadelphia played
game was dull and
only became inter
caught the home te
ninth inning. Long
by Stahl and Collin
then tied the score.
called on account of
6,494. Score:

Philadelphia.		
Cooley, c. f.	......	
Hallman, 2b	......	
Lajoie, 1b	......	
Delehanty, l. f.	......	
Geier, r. f.	......	
Clements, c.	......	
Gillen, s. s.	......	
Nash, 3b	......	
Taylor, p.	......	
Totals	......	

Boston.		
Hamilton, c. f.	....	
Tenney, 1b	....	
Long, s. s.	....	
Duffy, l. f.	....	
Stahl, r. f.	....	
Lowe, 2b	....	
Collins, 3b	....	
Ganzel, c.	....	
Lewis, p.	....	
*Klobedanz	....	
**Yeager	....	
Totals	....	

*Batted for Ganze
**Batted for Lew

Philadelphia .. 3 0
Boston 1 0

Earned runs—Ph
Two-base hits—Del

6

MAY 1897—*An earthquake shakes Cleveland, causing tall buildings to sway and glass windows to break in homes. Residents aren't wholly convinced it is an earthquake until Professor Morley of Adelbert College, now the administrative center of Case Western Reserve University, confirms it on his seismograph. An idea by Herbert Henry, a student at Case University, would blossom into one of the largest chemical companies in the world; on May 18, Dow began operations producing commercial chlorine. Globe Iron Works takes over the Cleveland Shipbuilding Company and two years later renames it the American Shipbuilding Company; in 1967 the American Shipbuilding Company would name George Steinbrenner III as its chief executive officer. In Cleveland parks and grassy fields, bluebirds are back in force. And tiny flowers called four-petal bluets blanket the grounds like a cerulean spring snow.*

* * * *

THE SOLUTION TO THE "INDIAN PROBLEM," as white America called its version of reform, was mostly twofold by the 1890s: wholesale conversion to Christianity, and "Americanization." Each reservation was assigned by the U.S. government a ministry of Christian denomination. There were no hard and fast rules for the selection of the denomination—it was a kind of lottery method. For the most part, the first step in conversion was to abolish all remnants of Native American spiritual beliefs. Sacred articles like pipes and bundled sweetgrass were gathered and burned in bonfires. Ornamental clothing and body dress like earrings were forbidden. Rituals were suppressed.

The Christian ministry also took on the job of education. This was not wholly an altruistic endeavor. The government ran some schools and subsidized others, and there was competition for funds. On urging the Church to build more Catholic Indian schools, the director of the Bureau of Catholic Indian Missions once said: "We do an immense deal of good, get the Indians into our hands and thus make them Catholics: if we neglect it any longer, the Government and the Protestants will build ahead of us schools in all the agencies and crowd us completely out and the Indians are lost."

On April 15, 1897, the U.S. Senate debated whether to increase appropriations to Catholic-run Indian schools. George Graham Vest, a Democratic senator from Missouri, had this to say about the issue: "If I had control of these schools I would give them to those who have studied the Indians; those who have taken the young Indians from the tepee, segregated them from their fathers and mothers and taught them the religion of Christ, even if the cross is the emblem of their religion. I would infinitely rather see them Catholics than savages."

Probably the most famous of the Indian schools was Carlisle in Pennsylvania. (Legendary coach "Pop" Warner began coaching at

Carlisle in 1897.) Founded by a former U.S. Army captain named Richard Pratt, Carlisle became the model for Indian schools. Children were ripped from their parents and brought hundreds, even thousands, of miles from home to attend the school. All vestiges of their Native life were torn away. Boys wore military-style outfits with high stiff collars, suspenders, and, most times, ill-fitting leather boots. Their long hair, in some tribes a symbol of manhood, was cut short. The girls wore simple Euro-American dresses. Christian names were assigned. Punishment was swift and severe. Children were beaten and kicked for such egregious sins as "speaking Indian." A five-dollar bounty was placed on runaways. Thousands died of disease and maltreatment.

Still, Pratt was a master of publicity. He commissioned "before and after" portraits of his students. In the before pictures the children were dressed in outrageous Native garb that usually had no connection to their tribes. The after pictures showed fresh-scrubbed faces and slicked-down hair. Pratt's phrase "Kill the Indian and save the man" became a rallying cry for Indian reformers. By the time Sockalexis entered the National League, there were nearly three hundred Indian schools across the country, most modeled on Carlisle, with some twenty-two thousand students—about 10 percent of the entire Indian population of the United States.

On May 8 the Cleveland Indians beat the Chicago White Stockings and evened their record at 6 and 6. They had won six of their last seven games and were the hottest team in the National League. The

Indian was the talk of the nation. The *New York Journal* printed this poem by R. K. Munkittrick on May 6, which read in part:

This is bounding Sockalexis
Fielder of the mighty Clevelands.

Like the catapult in action,
For the plate he throws the baseball,
Till the rooters, blithely rooting,
Shout until they shake the bleachers,
"Sockalexis, Sockalexis,
Sock it to them, Sockalexis!"

Like the bloom on the prairies,
Plunging from the flames up-leaping,
Snorting at the crimson billows
That his hinder members frizzle,
Till the condor notes the odor,
And his wings flap in the prescience
Of a rich and luscious banquet—
So spry Sockalexis capers,
Leaving far behind the whirlwind,
When he starts upon a home run.

Such is merry Sockalexis,
Who can bat and knock the home run,
Who can scalp the blooming umpire
Till the rooters in their glory

Knowing no fit terms of praise, all
Lift their voices: "Sockalexis,
Sockalexis, Sockalexis!"
Till the welkins madly spitting,
And the purple cave of echo
Sends back all the surging chorus:
"Sockalexis, Sockalexis,
Sock it to them, Sockalexis!"

On May 7, against Chicago, Sock went four-for-four with a triple and made at least two heart-stopping grabs in the outfield. The lead in the *Cleveland Plain Dealer* read:

> The man who said that there are no good Indians except dead Indians, or words to that effect, surely never saw one Louis Sockalexis, late of the Penobscot tribe, but now of the tribe of Tebeau. . . . The baseball fans who witnessed Sock's performance yesterday will agree that he is the best Indian that ever wandered down the pike. Pocahontas was never a marker to him and all the other good Indians of history fade into insignificance before the new found hero.

Cap Anson, the Chicago manager, had thrown a lefty against Cleveland in hopes of neutralizing the left-handed batting star. But at this point in his career the Indian could have gone four-for-four against a Winchester rifle.

The Indians were now one game out of second place, a position shared by Louisville and a surprising Pittsburgh team. The Orioles, however, looked like they would run away with the pennant, starting the season with a blistering 10 and 2 record. Baltimore's "Wee" Willie Keeler was in the midst of a hitting streak that would stretch to forty-four games (still a National League record, now shared with Pete Rose). Ned Hanlon, the manager of the Orioles, rotated four starting pitchers: Joe Corbett, Bill Hoffer, Arlie Pond, and Jerry Naps. In a league where most teams featured three front-line starters who each pitched upwards of four hundred innings, Hanlon's four-man rotation guarded against weary late-season arms. Still, no one was about to hand Baltimore the pennant, especially the Cleveland nine. There was, as sports hounds are fond of saying, a lot of baseball to be played.

When the Indians left the Windy City, they held their first winning record of the season, with seven wins against six loses. The team was playing enthusiastically and with confidence. "We are playing ball at last," Tebeau said in the *Plain Dealer*, "and I don't think anybody can stop us for long at a time. All we had to do was to strike our stride, and we were sure to be all right." The Indians were looking forward to an upcoming extended home stand. The eastern clubs—Brooklyn, Boston, Washington, and the New York Giants—were next up on the schedule. Tebeau told a Cleveland sportswriter that he expected Brooklyn to be the toughest team to beat.

Indian fever was sweeping Cleveland. When the team train pulled into Union Depot, some five hundred fans were waiting, including, according to the *Plain Dealer*, forty or fifty women on hand to view the Indian up close. This level of fairer-sex enthusiasm was unprecedented and raised more than a few Victorian eyebrows. But by modern perspective, you couldn't blame the lady fans. Dwarfing his teammates at nearly six feet and 190 pounds, solid as Carnegie steel, Sockalexis filled out every stitch of his uniform, not like the other scrawny players with their baggy uniform pants. His hair was raven-black to his shoulders. Where most of the players then had droopy mustaches, the Indian's face was as smooth as a sophomore's, his complexion like deep-red wine. A Cincinnati sportswriter described him like this: "Sockalexis is a most attractive young man. He has the racial features of the redskin, but in his civilian clothes he passes as a handsome fellow. . . . Tall, lithe, straight as an arrow, admirably proportioned, he is a most striking figure on the ball field."

And off the ball field too. Perhaps acquiring his fashion sense from his eastern college days, Sockalexis shunned the popular assembly-line ready-to-wear suits made by Cleveland's Joseph & Feiss. Instead he preferred tailor-made ensembles like those at Charles Wieber's on Detroit Avenue. He often sported a college sweater rakishly draped over his shoulders. He even had his long locks cut, perhaps at George Myers's barbershop in the Hollenden Hotel. A picture of sartorial splendor as he stepped from the train in the dingy surroundings of Union Depot, the Indian made quite an impression on the ladies of Cleveland.

At League Park the Brooklyn Bridegrooms took the first game, 3–2, proving Tebeau's prediction correct. Cleveland had a chance to tie the contest in the ninth with the Indian on third and one out.

Harry Blake hit a soft grounder to the right side, and Tebeau, coaching along the third base line, waved the Indian home. The throw to the plate just beat the hard-charging rookie. Though the loss stung, there were encouraging signs. Cy Young pitched well, scattering eight hits. His ankle was finally fully recovered. And though the rookie right fielder uncharacteristically committed an error that resulted in a Brooklyn run (in the seventh he rushed a ground single by Brooklyn's third baseman Billy Shindle and the ball went under his glove and through his legs), at the plate Sockalexis was still ripping the cover off the ball. In the fourth he hit a screaming line drive that hit just six inches from the top of the right field fence; the ball hit the wall with such ferocity that it bounced halfway back to the infield and the Indian trotted into third base for a triple.

For the first time that season, there was a palpable energy at League Park. You could tell by the way the players snapped the ball to one another during warm-ups. You could see it in the determined looks on their faces. There was an upbeat feeling in the stands. Fans were arriving for the games early. They cheered in full throat. The Indian was electric to watch. The town of Cleveland had a baseball legend in the making.

Unlike the Baltimore Orioles, the Boston Beaneaters started the season disappointingly, with only one victory in seven games. They suffered pitching problems as two of their starters, Jack Stivetts and Jim Sullivan, had sore arms. But as their train pulled into Cleveland, and despite the mound trouble, they had begun to play good ball. One theory is that the team had responded to a tongue-lashing by the straitlaced Beaneaters owner, Arthur Soden, who had had enough of dirty play throughout the league, and especially by his club. He refused to pay any fines levied by umpires against his players, a common practice then for ownership. Whether Soden's tongue-lashing had anything to do with the team's turnaround is debatable, but the team that played the Indians in mid-May was much better than the one that began the season.

While Sockalexis was etching his name into records and lore, the game in Cleveland was spurting along, as Robison and the ministers battled over the Sabbath. To Sockalexis, the controversy was a matter of getting another day to leap around League Park. He went to church on Sundays as a child, and even if he continued formal worship during his time in the National League, it's doubtful he thought obeying the Sabbath meant not playing baseball. But like the rest of the players, Sockalexis stayed out of politics and went to work when he was told to. On the first two Sundays of the home stand, he was told to stay home.

The general consensus was that Robison would at some point challenge city authorities to enforce the contentious blue law (Sunday closings) as it pertained to baseball. On May 14 he announced that he intended to do just that. In the revised statutes of Ohio, the law was listed under the Act of April 9, 1881, volume 78, page 126, section 7032A. It read in part: "Whoever on the first day of the week, commonly called Sunday, participates in or exhibits to the public in any grounds, garden or other place in this state *** any baseball playing *** he, or she, shall on complaint made within twenty days thereafter, be fined. . . ." The law went on to state that arrests could be made following a complaint to the proper authorities, and only after the act. Robison and his team of legal counsel interpreted this as meaning that the team could be arrested, but only after the contest on the field had been decided.

In a long explanation of his intentions printed in the *Plain Dealer,* Robison said: "If anyone sees fit to test the law he may cause arrest after the game has been played, and then we will test it in all the courts there are." In this game of high stakes poker, Robison was hedging his bet. On the table was the gate receipts for an expected full League Park, and Robison was promising the fans a full nine innings or more of baseball. Though Robison was playing with an inferior hand, the magnate thought the authorities would never act on such an unpopular ordinance. They certainly wouldn't arrest his now popular team in front of a park filled with cranks. If he could get away with one game, then his chances of holding all the chips—playing every Sunday—were that much better.

Robison also had his suspicions about the ministers' motivation. Were they truly acting in service of the Lord? Or was there another motivation? By the 1890s, for the most part, Protestant churches in Cleveland represented the moneyed elite, while the burgeoning working-class immigrants found their spiritual guidance in the Catholic Church. Though Sunday baseball games might have been the point of contention, the clash represented a much bigger power struggle.

In 1870, Cleveland was home to fourteen parishes. By the turn of the twentieth century, that number had risen to more than fifty. Though anti-Catholic sentiment in Cleveland had reached its zenith in the 1850s, it was still very much alive in 1897. The *Cleveland Leader* newspaper led the anti-Catholic crusade in print. Though Cleveland's big money backed the Protestants, a fast flow of small money was making the Catholics a viable threat. The same workingmen whose wives nudged them as the collection plate was passed were the ones who took Robison's streetcars to League Park. Drawn by Protestant ministers, Sunday baseball was a line in the sand, and Robison had no doubt that the ministers cared more about the loss of influence, power, and cash flow than any higher calling. He also knew that the ministers of Cleveland wouldn't give in easily.

Boston swept the series against the Indians and began to rise to the top of the standings, a position they would hold with ferocity. Washington was next up for Cleveland, and Robison brashly scheduled a Sunday game. The day of the game, with the attending publicity, League Park was packed with nearly ten thousand fans spilling from the stands to circle the field, and thousands more who couldn't gain admission gathered at the Lexington Avenue gate. Robison had to smile. Not even the Indian's now bankable drawing power could come close to the circus that surrounded the baseball magnate and his crusade.

Robison was smart enough to issue rain checks (there might have been a riot had he not). But he also put extra streetcars on his Lexington Avenue line, and game or no game there would be no refunds on fares. Though the game wasn't scheduled to start until 3 P.M., by 9:30 cranks were hanging from the trolleys. And it wasn't only Robison who profited from the event. Registers in city hotels sagged with wet fountain ink. There wasn't a table to be had in a Cleveland restaurant. The pitch was feverous. From the dining room at the Hollenden Hotel, to the shanty Irish saloons on Whiskey Island, Robison and his crusade was the heated topic of conversation. No matter what was to happen that afternoon, the magnate had scored a coup, with public opinion running heavily on his side. The police had issued notice that they would enforce the law to the fullest extent. They had even given Robison their itinerary. When he heard of their intentions, the magnate wasn't happy. But by then there was nothing he could do.

In the top of the first, when a lazy fly nestled in the Indian's glove for the third out, Captain English of the Cleveland police strode to the center of the diamond and announced to umpire Tim Hurst that he was under arrest. Fearing an all-out riot, scores of uniformed cops circled the field. But the patrons on hand were, for the most part, well behaved. Many were not hardened cranks and simply attended the game to witness the sideshow. The police presence, however, added to the drama, and fans booed lustily as Hurst was escorted from the field. In a brilliant stoke of strategy, Captain English, an avid crank himself, led the force of police. English took a great deal of razzing from his pals in the stands. Still, as he led the procession of players from the field he kept his head up and his icebreaker chin jutted. Sportswriters and news reporters ran ahead to the Central Police Station to be on hand when the paddy wagons arrived. Opting for his own form of transportation, Cleveland catcher Chief Zimmer rode his bicycle and arrived ahead of everyone else.

Hundreds of baseball fans hooted and howled as police led the players, and Tim Hurst, up the stairs to the stationhouse. Inside, Zimmer was already being booked—given a "ticket" actually, as Robison had already posted bond. Engaging in a bit of gamesmanship, the Cleveland players shouldered their way in front of the Washington club to sign the blotter. Most of the banter between cops and ballplayers was good natured. Only Sockalexis seemed uncomfortable; perhaps the still-fresh memory of the South Bend jail brought a taste of bile to his mouth. "He looked like a whipped kitten," wrote one newsman. The reporter went on: "To think of a big Indian being captured by a city bluecoat without having made at least a little struggle to save his scalp was perhaps different from the ordinary manner of procedure in that neck of the woods from whence he came."

But Sockalexis soon realized that the proceedings were not as dire as he first thought, and a "good natured smile" formed on his lips as he watched his teammates' lighthearted manner. "Well I can stand it in good form if you can," Sock pronounced, as he looked over the happy crowd of fellow ballplayers. He gave his age as twenty-three, which drew more than one guffaw from the peanut gallery, as it was common knowledge that he signed as a twenty-seven-year-old rookie. "If he had been hanging by the neck since he was twenty-three years old he would have been dead long ago," remarked a constable within earshot of a reporter.

Despite the public relations coup, Robison couldn't have been entirely happy. The hand he played had cost him a five-thousand-dollar gate, and the show of force from city officials meant that the ministers were not afraid to brandish their clout. The future of Sunday baseball in Cleveland was very much in doubt.

Though Robison was convinced that his battle was solely against the Protestant ministers, the next day's *Plain Dealer* trumpeted a conspiracy theory of a third party lurking in the background. According to the story, it was Cleveland's liquor league, an association of saloon owners with considerable influence in city politics, who forced the cops to act. The motivation of the saloon owners was of course financial—to the tune of ten thousand or so customers who would spend their Sundays at League Park instead of in Cleveland saloons. The liquor league was a powerful lobby, strong enough to circumvent Cleveland's blue laws.

It was something of an unholy alliance—the ministers and the liquor league. But the ministers were smart enough to know that battling Sunday baseball was one thing, and taking the Sunday glass of whiskey from the exploding immigrant population was quite another. The clergy was smart enough to fight the battles they could win.

If the saloons of Cleveland were a subversive enemy of Robison, for Sockalexis they were as friendly as an old college chum. In the smoky Cleveland barrooms that littered the area around League Park, friends were made in the time it took to pour a shot of whiskey. Surrounded by sportswriters and fans in straw boater hats and crisp starched collars, the Indian felt a level of acceptance and equality, albeit false. For the new baseball star, the booze was free and flowed endlessly. Life was a big party, one where entrance was gained by celebrity status. And he played the role to the hilt. He smoked Cuban cigars. He astounded his following with his knowledge of classic literature: a passage from *The Iliad*, a line from Shakespeare. Sober, he was polite and shy with all the natural insecurities of one who didn't fit in but wanted to desperately. With the aid of bourbon, those insecurities disappeared. Bourbon made him forget he was different, forget he was an Indian.

On May 31 the Indians headed east to play Brooklyn. The curtain had come down on the first act of Sunday baseball, but the drama was far from over. The road trip would take them to Boston, Washington, Baltimore, and back to New York to play the Giants. Cleveland was in the thick of the race, having climbed to fifth place with a record of 18–13. They trailed league-leading Baltimore by only five games. The eastern swing would make or break their season. It would also bring the Indian onto the biggest stage in sports: New York's Polo Grounds.

The weather in Brooklyn was miserable. Early that morning fat balls of rain splattered on the field at Eastern Park. By midday the rain had eased, but a thick fog had descended, enveloping the field. A doubleheader was scheduled, but with the field a quagmire, the morning game was out of the question and the afternoon match was in serious doubt. For Bridegrooms management this was unfortunate. Memorial Day always ensured a big gate. But this

Memorial Day was special. The Indian was making his debut in Brooklyn.

Eastern Park was bordered on two sides by trolley tracks, and the team was euphemistically called the Trolley Dodgers, which was later shortened to Dodgers. In typical Brooklyn fashion, the nickname was not of the most flattering stripe. It was a term to describe individuals who jumped on moving trolleys to avoid paying the fare. But in the 1890s, the Brooklyn nine were better known as the Bridegrooms, after four of the stars on the 1888 team were married during the season.

The Bridegrooms were in the middle of the standings, with a .500 record. The Brooklyn fans were loyal and rabid, with attendance growing each year. But the team had not won the pennant since 1890, and the fans were running out of patience. The team's star was Fielder Jones, who batted a blistering .354 in 1896. His performance that season had fans prophesizing, "Wait 'til next year," perhaps the first utterance of that famous Brooklyn lament.

As if Brooklyn management's prayers were answered, the dense fog lifted just after noon. A warm sun burned away the last gray wisps and dried the field to the point where it was passable if not truly playable. In spite of the daunting weather, the crowd began lining up at the park entrance in the early afternoon. By game time, about 2 P.M., cranks filled every seat, with thousands of them spilling out along the first- and third-base lines just in foul territory. In those days the visiting team shared the gate with the home club. Although the allure of seeing Sockalexis was not responsible for every paid admission, he was undeniably the main attraction.

When the gate was counted, more than eighteen thousand had paid to get in—the largest crowd then in Brooklyn baseball history. In just one day the Indian had earned his salary for the next two seasons.

"Bald" Billy Barnie, the manager of the Bridegrooms, no doubt believing the rumors of the Indian's susceptibility to lefty pitching, started a southpaw. Harley Payne was a lanky six-footer in his second year in the majors. Though right-handed batters had their way with Payne, his roundhouse delivery was especially tough to hit from the left side of the plate. But Barnie should have known better. Having coached at Yale before joining the Bridegrooms, Barnie had watched Sockalexis tear up left-handed college pitching. Though as a manager for Louisville and Washington, Barnie was a combined 86–171, he was considered one of the best baseball minds of his day. He insisted on fundamental baseball strategy that is still employed: throwing to the cutoff man, moving runners along with sacrifice. He seemed to hedge his strategic move before the game: "[Sockalexis] is a wonder at all points of the game," the manager said.

The fickle Brooklyn crowd gave the home team a hero's welcome as they splashed onto the field. Brooklyn had just itself returned from a western trip, and the crowd was hungry for baseball and more than curious about the new Cleveland right fielder. Four times the Indian stepped to the plate to face Payne. Four times the crowd rose to its feet, stomping the bleachers in a thunderous cadence accompanied by the now familiar war whoop. Four times the Indian scalded the ball. But each time the ball found a Bridegroom mitt. Hard-hit outs are still outs, and Barnie looked like a genius. In the field, however, the Indian made a play that was worth the price of admission.

In the middle of a Bridegrooms rally in the first, Brooklyn's Shindle stepped to the plate. Shindle always carried a good luck charm in the back pocket of his uniform. "It was taken from the hind foot of a rabbit shot in a cemetery at midnight by a red-bearded coon," he once explained. With Jones on second, Shindle ripped a liner to right-center. Sure the ball could not be caught, Jones sprinted toward third. But neither Jones's intuition nor Shindle's rabbit's foot was a match for the Indian's speed. In full gallop he caught the ball, then turned and fired toward second; only a questionable "homer" call allowed Jones to find his way safely back to the bag. Even the rowdy Brooklyn fans appreciated the play. According to a story in the *New York Journal,* the local cranks called out, "Sox, you're a peach," and that "Sox, grinning contently, took off his cap and bowed his respects to the vast assemblage before which he had made his big eastern debut." Brooklyn managed two runs off Cy Young in the first, then three in the second. It was all they would need. Cleveland started the all-important road trip with a 5–2 defeat.

In the second contest of the series, Sockalexis was on the bench as the game started, Blake in his place in right field. Perhaps Tebeau was protecting his star rookie from the rowdy Brooklyn crowd, or maybe he had a premonition that it wasn't Sock's day. The Indian would, however, see action in the game. In the third inning the Brooklyn center fielder, Mike Griffin, hit a tremendous drive to deep center. Cleveland's Jimmy McAleer raced after the ball. As he began to dive for the catch, he lost his footing on the still slippery grass and tumbled hard to the ground. The crowd hushed as McAleer lay motionless on the outfield grass. For several minutes the center fielder was unconscious. Players from both teams carried McAleer from the field. Tebeau moved Blake to center and waved Sockalexis into the game.

The crowd, disappointed in the Indian's absence in the starting lineup, stood and cheered. The good-natured rookie doffed his cap. The cheers, however, quickly turned derisive. Sock responded in the eighth inning by smacking a double into the gap in right-center field, driving in two runs to put his team ahead by one. But Sock would make a rookie mistake in the ninth that would cost Cleveland the game. With two Bridegrooms on the bases and one out, Griffin scaled one down the right field line. Sockalexis retrieved the ball in the corner. Instead of throwing to the infield to cut off the go-ahead run, he tried to gun the lead runner down at the plate. Though the throw easily beat the runner home, it sailed high over Zimmer's outstretched glove and both runners scored, sealing for Brooklyn the victory. The Indian ran from the field with his head down as the crowd howled at his mistake.

There is no way to calculate the loneliness Sockalexis felt in unfriendly territory like Brooklyn, or even in his adopted home of Cleveland. Whether he cried in the bath or alone in a hotel room. There's no way of knowing whether he shoved the taunts deep under a smiling exterior or took out his frustration with a ferocious swing or a diving catch, or just spilled them to a sympathetic prostitute or into a glass of whiskey. There's no way of knowing, except his life tells us in varying ways that he probably did all of these things.

The Indian's arrival in New York was featured in the local sports pages. The front page, however, told of a deadly outbreak among the Cheyenne in Montana. The Indian wars had decimated the once proud tribe. Backed onto reservations, nearly starving, the tribe relied on U.S. government relief for basic staples. A sheep rancher was killed, allegedly by a Cheyenne. Reports then filtered back east that as many as twelve whites had been murdered, including five soldiers from a "colored" cavalry company stationed at Fort Custer. In the following day's papers, the story grew. The *New York Evening Times* headline read: "Indian Outbreak Feared." The Indian wars might have been over, but resentment still lingered and the story still sold papers.

The only thing that mattered to Sockalexis, though, was that the team was heading to Boston. He was going home for the first time in quite a while.

INDIAN OUTBREAK FEARED

Cheyennes Said to Have Murdered Settlers in Southern Montana and Killed Five Colored Troopers.

WHITES GREATLY ALARMED

Dispatches from Montana Conveying This Information Are Discredited at the War and Interior Departments—Situation Not Serious.

HELENA, Mon., May 31.—The Cheyenne Indians are reported on the war path, and are said to have killed almost a dozen men, including five United States soldiers. The Indians have no reservation of their own, but roam over the southern part of the State near the Crow Reservation. The white settlers are in arms, and the women and children are being sent into the northern towns for safety.

The Cheyennes make Lame Deer Agency their headquarters. Hoover, a sheep herder, was recently shot while herding sheep, and it was proved that Indians did it. He was killed because he caught several Indians killing sheep.

Two companies of colored cavalry from Custer were ordered to the agency Wednesday, and on Saturday a courier arrived from the agency with information that George Walter, the Postmaster, and Lou Alderson, a stock man, had been shot and killed; also that the Indians had fired upon the cavalry and killed five, and had sixty cowboys surrounded. The cavalry from Fort Keogh and a company of infantry left Saturday for the scene.

There are certainly grounds for fear. The Cheyennes are determined, and they are being reinforced by renegade Crows. Rosebud ranchers received a consignment of rifles and ammunition at this point to-day. Ranchmen and stockmen have organized at Cheyenne agency and demanded the Indians who killed Hoover. The names of the Indians are known and they are protected by fifty bucks. Sheriff Gibbs and Coroner Bateman have returned from Barringer's Ranch, in the neighborhood of which the inquest was held on the body of Hoover. The verdict charged the Cheyenne Indians with his murder.

While the inquest was proceeding, sixty men under James Brown arrived on their way to the agency. The Sheriff pleaded with them to return, and told them that sixty of them against 400 or 500 Indians, armed and such fighters as the Che—

Cheyennes has reached the Interior Department, and the Indian officials are at a loss to account for the lack of advices, if any trouble has occurred or is apprehended. In view of the lack of official advices, the fact that the agency is in close telegraphic communication and that the agency is in charge of an experienced army officer, no alarm or uneasiness for the safety of the people in that section is felt. No incidents have been reported to the department recently that would likely lead to serious results, and the fact that the reports date the trouble several days back is cited as significant.

NO OFFICIAL NEWS.

Secretary of War Has Received No Information of the Outbreak.

WEST POINT, May 31.—Secretary of War Alger, when asked to-day about the Indian outbreak in Montana, said that he had no information whatever in regard to the matter. He has received no official news of an Indian outbreak. Adjt. Gen. Ruggles also said that he had received no recent news, though about a week ago, he said, the bodies of two white men were found, and two troops of cavalry were sent out from Fort Keogh to investigate the matter.

WOMAN KILLED BY MISTAKE.

She Received the Bullet Intended for the Man She Was Trying to Shield.

Virginia Johnson, a negress, was killed last night with a pistol bullet in the court between the front and rear houses at 533 West Forty-second Street. Her death was through mischance. Austin Stewart pulled the trigger of a revolver aimed at Edward Roe, with whom Virginia lived, just as she sprang between them, and she was shot in the heart.

Roe and Stewart, both negroes, quarreled over a game of craps, and words led to blows. Roe received a slap in the face and had drawn a knife when Stewart pulled out his weapon, and the interposition of the woman and her death occurred in a few moments.

Although Stewart saw the result of his first shot, he was either fearful of Roe's knife or determined to punish him for drawing it on him, as he deliberately fired a second shot, wounding Roe in the back. Leaving the dead woman and Roe, Stewart went to his room, on the third floor of the rear house, put on his best clothes and prepared to escape. He was arrested as he was leaving the place, and locked up in the West Forty-seventh Street Station House. Roe was taken to the Roosevelt Hospital. The bullet was extracted. He will recover. The woman's body was sent to the Morgue.

SAFE BLOWERS IN BROOKLYN.

The Reward Was Not Commensurate with the Risk Incurred.

The office of John J. Burns, a florist, in Meeker Avenue, near the Penny Bridge, Brooklyn, was visited by burglars yesterday morning, and the safe blown open. The

7

JUNE 1897—*In Washington, D.C., the United States Senate is finalizing legislation that would annex Hawaii. In Havana, famed artist Frederic Remington wires William Randolph Hearst saying that there would be no war in Cuba; Hearst reportedly wires back: "Please remain. You supply the pictures, I'll supply the war." George Ferris's new invention draws the young and old alike to amusement parks across the country. Euclid Beach Park is a popular summer spot for Clevelanders. The Hiram House in Cleveland offers the first of that city's Americanization classes in such subjects as citizenship and vocational education. The city is split on the issue; some embrace the "melting pot" theory of allowing different ethnicities to mix, while others seek a policy of Anglo conformity. Burrows Stationery and Bookseller expands, opening at a new location on Euclid Avenue; their biggest seller is* The Jesuit Relations and Allied Documents, 1610–1791, *a compilation of Jesuit letters that details the first European contact with American Indians in Maine. In a Cleveland courthouse, Frank Robison's lawyers defend his team's right to play Sunday ball.*

* * * *

IN A SEASON AND A LEAGUE filled with player brawls, player and umpire arrests, and fan riots, Boston was the exception. The Goody Two-shoes nature of the Beaneaters must have made a dead rabble-rouser like King Kelly spike the top of his coffin. The Beaneaters owner, Arthur Soden, and his field manager, Frank Selee, had iron-fisted styles. Soden was the quintessential baseball dictator. In 1879 he fathered the reserve clause that gave owners complete control of players' rights. Selee would replace even the most popular players without a second thought if it made his team stronger. Like Bald Barnie of the Bridegrooms, Selee was an innovator and a stickler for fundamentals. Infielders thrived under Selee's tutelage, with the double play being his hallmark. Later in his career, Selee coached the Chicago Cubs and perhaps the most famous double play combination in baseball history: Tinkers to Evers to Chance. Selee also had a knack for spotting talent. The 1897 Beaneaters featured pitcher Kid Nichols, who in his previous seven years with Boston had five thirty-plus-win seasons; outfielder Hugh Duffy, who in 1894 hit an amazing .440; and third baseman Jimmy Collins, considered one of the best to ever play that position.

Having lost both games of the rain-shortened series against Brooklyn, the Cleveland team's immediate future wasn't looking any brighter. Boston was in the midst of a seventeen-game winning streak. Over the course of June they went an incredible 22–2. The castlelike grandstand of South End Grounds, the Beaneaters' field, might not have seemed the friendliest of stops for most of the Indians, but it was a welcome sight for Sockalexis.

Just south of Boston is the city of Worcester and Holy Cross College. Here for the Indian were warm memories of a simpler time. He was campus hero, with little pressure and loads of fun. For the first time that season, the Indian had struggled at the plate in Brooklyn. Much of his inadequacy was due to the razzing of the extremely vocal Brooklynites. Though he seemed to have put to rest the rumor of his inability to hit a curveball, pitchers throughout the league were gunning for him. Teammate Harry Blake described Sock's situation to a Cleveland sportswriter: "He is batting as strong as ever," Blake said, "but he has a harder proposition to go against. There has been so much talk about Socks that the pitchers are all after him and pitch harder for him than for any man on the team." Blake went on to tell the sportswriter that the abuse from fans and opposing players against the Indian was "something awful."

The first game of the Boston series lasted only two innings because of heavy rain. Despite the weather, the park was packed, and the fans were every bit as vocal and negative as those in Brooklyn. The headline in the sports section of the *Boston Globe* read: "Indian in Right Field," the story accompanied by a cartoon that made Sockalexis into something of a Greek god. Though a small contingent of Penobscots made the trip down from Maine, and a larger group of Holy Cross students and teammates were present, their support was drowned out by the Boston faithful. These were the loyal fans of King Kelly and George Armstrong Custer. For Sockalexis, South End Grounds was not Indian territory. Still, Sock responded in the only way he knew: In the rain-shortened affair he

127

came to the plate twice, and twice he hammered clean base hits. There seemed a fiercer purpose to his at bats. It was as though he was feeding off the negative energy hurled toward him from the bleachers. He also seemed to enjoy the glare of the spotlight, and in Boston the spotlight was white-hot.

The week that Sockalexis and the rest of the team were in Boston, this piece ran in the *Boston Traveler*:

> In recent years there has been no ball player who has attracted so much attention in Boston as Sockalexis, and, judging from his work of yesterday, he deserves all the good things which have been said of him. As a swatter of the ball, there are few men who will make a finer record this year than the Indian.
>
> He goes up to the plate with the air of a man whose [*sic*] going to punch the ball out of sight or of grip of any fielder. He respects the pitchers personally, but he has the air of a man who is very well satisfied that curves of high and low degree were simply intended for him to slaughter.
>
> It is really worth the price of admission to see Sockalexis on his way to first base. I never saw a deer run, but if a deer can run as fast as Sockalexis, then I can understand what a tough time my hunting friends have annually in the Maine woods. Each season the league generally produces something in the way of a sensation. This year, the sensation is Sockalexis, and the chances are that he will grow greater as he becomes more seasoned. And I cannot help but think it a shame that Sockalexis doesn't wear a Boston uni-

form. He would be a tremendous favorite in this city, and there was a time when the Boston management could have easily enough secured him. But we must not expect too much from our management. Now that the nine is playing pennant ball, they simply look wise and take in the dough.

Ah, dough, that is a great thing, and we must have it to live, but the Boston magnates could quite easily afford to give up some of the strawberry shortcake it gets on holidays for a man like Sockalexis. He is a good Indian, a mighty big chief among the great medicine men, and our bonnets are off to him.

That same week, *Sporting Life* called him the best-throwing out-fielder in baseball, "barring no one." The *Boston Post* wrote that the huge crowd at the park was due to the Indian's presence:

> The lone brave Louis Sockalexis, the tall and muscular Indian who only a few years ago was hopscotching all over the state with the Holy Cross team, made his bow before a Boston audience. . . . The first time up the rooters began the Indian war whoop, which apparently strengthened Louis' courage, for he batted out a single, and his second time up he planted one in the same place.

The *Boston Herald* described Sockalexis as "finely built" and a player in possession of remarkable ease and grace. "As a fielder, he covers a great deal of ground and is a sure catch. . . . His is a left-handed hitter, and bats very freely and strongly, beside being a splendid hand at bunting." The *Herald* went on to say that

Sockalexis spent his time after the game "acknowledging the salutations of his friends." It is not clear in the article if this was meant as a euphemism for his carousing that night in Boston, but it certainly seemed that the whole team played with a hangover the next day. The Indians were down 14–3 at the end of the second inning and lost the game by a score of 21–8. The second game of the three-game series was postponed because of rain, and the last game was mercifully shortened, with Cleveland losing 8–1.

Though Sockalexis had two hits in the rained-out first game, he seemed to lose his confidence at the plate in Boston. Perhaps it was nerves, playing in front of his family, childhood friends, and college chums. Or perhaps he wasn't all that comfortable in the spotlight. More likely it was the hospitality of the Boston saloons that slowed his bat. Sock's return home was not at all triumphant, and he and the other Cleveland players had to be relieved to be heading to Washington.

In those first two weeks of June, the entire eastern seaboard was soaked by rain. The series against Washington was supposed to be three games, but they were fortunate to get two in. The Senators were at the bottom of the National League, and the Indians were lucky to draw them after the trouncing they took in Boston. Cleveland responded with two victories in the capital. The team was two games over .500 and still alive in the race for the pennant—at least that was the belief of some of the Cleveland faithful. In the *Cleveland Plain Dealer* there was a story of one hardened fan who had wagered a thousand dollars with the paper's editor that the Indians would take the flag. He would know soon enough how wise a bet he made. The team train rolled out of the capital en route to Baltimore. The club that sat atop the National League was next—the hated Orioles.

The rematch of the previous year's Temple Cup combatants went as expected: Baseball spikes were used as weapons, and pitchers threw high and tight fastballs with alarming regularity. Pure and simple, these two teams didn't like each other. Poor McDonald drew umpiring duties and was the target of the most vile invectives. In the final game of the three-game series, Patsy Tebeau again had to be pulled off the umpire by teammates after a questionable call. The crowd was whipped to fever pitch. After each game, hundreds of drunken louts waited for the Indians to leave the park. And after each game, a platoon of Baltimore's finest escorted the team from the field to their omnibus.

Sockalexis was the prime target of the taunting, and Baltimore's John McGraw played provocateur. Just before the first game started, the Baltimore third bagger came onto the field wearing a full Indian war bonnet with feathers reaching down below the seat of his baggy baseball pants. The crowd went insane, serenading their captain with an Indian war chant. In the following two games, taking McGraw's lead, war bonnets were the fashion of choice in the stands. Each time Sockalexis came to the plate, the fans rose and in unison repeated the war chant, the sound like a Florida State football rally in a bowl game.

Sockalexis responded by making a series of spectacular throws from the outfield, including one that nailed McGraw at the plate. As the Baltimore captain brushed himself off, he stared out to right field in disbelief. Indeed, the Indian's athletic prowess stunned many. Newspaper reports during spring training had him doing a standing flip à la Ozzie Smith. He was also adroit on the parallel bars and other gymnastic equipment. In a time when muscle and body control were not all that prevalent in baseball, Sockalexis was like nothing the other players had ever seen.

Despite the circuslike atmosphere and the dirty looks, the series was a sparkling exhibition of baseball. For Cleveland, third baseman Bobby Wallace seemed to swallow every ball hit in his direction. On the Baltimore side, several times infielders Hughie Jennings (who later became the longtime manager of the Detroit Tigers) and Heinie Reitz combined on brilliant double plays to snuff out Cleveland rallies. Though Baltimore won the first two contests, 11–6 and 4–0, the games were a lot tighter than the scores indicate, and neither team gave up until the final out was called.

Tebeau didn't take losing to any team well, but he especially despised losing to the Orioles. He wasn't alone. It seemed the whole of the National League was on his side. " 'Anything to down the Orioles' is the slogan in the cities of the major league circuit outside of Orioletown," said an article in the *Washington Post* that week. But the story continued with a lament that Baltimore might just be too tough to beat: "About the only thing that can do the downing is a tornado or a pile driver. The Orioles positively refuse to be crushed. . . ."

If the first two games were well played, the third and final one was a showpiece. Baltimore held the early lead, 2–0, but Cleveland clawed back with two runs in the fourth on a triple by Sockalexis. The Indians gained the lead by scratching out single runs in the fifth and eighth. Cleveland scored the runs by implementing the best of "scientific baseball." On the base paths, Sock was a terror, stealing at will. Twice he stole second standing up.

Cleveland threatened to put the game away in the visitor's eighth. With Jimmy McAleer and Tebeau on base, Sockalexis smoked a liner to the opposite field. The Baltimore left fielder, Joe Kelley, who many years later would have a bronze plaque in his likeness hanging in Cooperstown, made an implausible catch. Tebeau, the lead runner, was so sure the ball was over Kelley's head that he had streaked home and was on his way to the bench when the double play was made, ending the rally. Still, his team held the lead going into the ninth.

But the bounces had not been kind to the Cleveland nine in Baltimore. The Orioles loaded the bases on a bloop single and two Baltimore chops (Oriole players, especially Willie Keeler, would hit down on the ball, bouncing it off the hard surface just in front of home plate or the plate itself). Though he had pitched heroically, Nig Cuppy was tiring. He walked in the tying run, and then, with none out, he had to face McGraw. There was utter bedlam in the stands, the fans shouting for blood. On the first pitch, McGraw too tried to chop it, but the ball was driven too far in front of the plate and it bounded to Wallace at third. Though he had been nearly flawless in the series, Wallace fumbled the play and the winning run scored easily.

Tebeau kicked the ground near first and stormed from the field, accompanied by taunts from the bleachers. Things were not good. His team was now one game below .500, in the middle of the pack, and three games further behind the Orioles in the standings. He knew it was only June, but if the Indians lost any more ground, making the championship series was pure fantasy. To make matters worse, the rowdy crowd that had faced the team after each game had grown in strength. A beer bottle and several rocks were thrown at the retreating Clevelanders. Tebeau, his French-Canadian temper boiling over, had taken all he was going to take. He rushed toward the angry mob, and only a quicker Sockalexis, who headed the manager off, saved Tebeau from bodily harm. As the team made its retreat from the ballpark, Tebeau shook his head. At least things couldn't get much worse, he must have thought.

Meanwhile, in Cleveland, the fate of Sunday baseball was being hashed out in city court. Robison and his lawyers had already won a victory of sorts with the local judiciary. Only one Cleveland player would stand trial, allowing the rest of the team to continue their National League schedule. The chosen representative was John Powell, a seldom-used substitute player.

The proceedings had bogged down over the lettering of the law. Robison's attorneys argued that the statute clearly stated that no baseball *game* should be played, and that as the police stopped the contest in the first inning a game—a full game—had not taken place. If this flimsy argument was a stall tactic, it worked. Even the jury took its time to decide. For some thirty-six hours they deliberated in a small room in the Cleveland courthouse. After an overnight without sleep, they finally found Powell guilty of violating state law prohibiting Sunday baseball. Robison's lawyers immediately filed a petition for appeal.

On June 1, under the headline "On the Warpath," the *Plain Dealer* reported that Cheyenne braves in Tongue River, Montana, had white settlers fleeing for their lives as bands of marauding Indian warriors terrorized the countryside. For a short time, America was transfixed again by a story that brought back the glory of the first frontier, the one before baseball.

In 1874, twenty-three years before Sockalexis put on a Cleveland uniform, the United States 7th Cavalry, disregarding the federal government's treaty with the Sioux and Cheyenne tribes, ventured into the Black Hills of the Dakota Territory. While there, they unexpectedly found gold, the news prompting a rush of fortune hunters. Two years later the 7th Cavalry, led by General George Armstrong Custer, returned to Dakota, this time to protect white prospectors from Indian resistance. Specifically, the army had ordered Custer to subdue, by any means, the Sioux leaders Sitting Bull and Crazy Horse. On June 24, Custer's troops located the Indian camp on the Little Bighorn River. The following day, greatly underestimating the Indian numbers, Custer and 225 of his soldiers attacked the camp.

Fourteen years later, on December 29, 1890, some 350 Sioux camped on the banks of Wounded Knee Creek in South Dakota. Earlier that fall the Sioux had begun a ritual called the Ghost

Dance. The practice started when the Sioux sent emissaries to Nevada to hear a Paiute shaman preach a new mysticism. The prophecies included the Indian dead rising from their graves and joining the living in a land again filled with buffalo, and an eruption of soil that would bury the white man and return the prairie to its once pristine beauty. On their return to South Dakota, the Sioux representatives preached the shaman's words. Soon the reservation was alive with Sioux wearing brightly colored "ghost shirts" emblazoned with images of eagles and buffalo. Their belief was that the shirts would protect them from cavalry bullets. The federal government in Washington, D.C., received word of the activity at Wounded Knee and ordered the arrest of Sitting Bull at the nearby Standing Rock Reservation. On December 15 the great Sioux chief was killed in the attempt. Two weeks later the army surrounded the Indian encampment at Wounded Knee.

From Custer's Last Stand to the massacre of Sioux at Wounded Knee, periodic outbreaks in the dwindling Indian wars had dominated America's news. They had everything a great news story should have: larger-than-life heroes, bloody fighting, mysterious enemies, and a misguided sense of right and wrong.

By the late 1890s a somewhat romantic revisionism had taken place. The Indian wars were becoming a distant memory. The Indian had become a nostalgic figure, representative of a rugged and simpler time. But white America had a funny way of celebrating this image. In April of 1897, Buffalo Bill's Wild West show with its "100 Indian warriors" played to sold-out crowds in New York's Madison Square Garden. That same year, a traveling "circus," as it was called, fielded an all-Indian baseball team and, like a fore-runner to the Harlem Globetrotters, toured the country. The team wore headdresses and other traditional Native garb. The white owner of the team, Guy Green, capitalized further on the stereo-type by publishing a book, *Fun and Frolic with an Indian Ball Team.*

By the late 1890s Indians themselves had organized semipro-fessional teams and, riding the curiosity factor of white America, held barnstorming tours throughout the Midwest, charging ad-mission along the way. The marketing of the American Indian co-incided with the phenomenal growth in the popularity of baseball. In some ways, newsprint about baseball filled the void left by the ending of the Indian wars. As far as the sportswriters were con-cerned, Sockalexis's timing was exquisite. An Indian playing base-ball—it couldn't get any better. These were the days of P. T. Barnum and Pulitzer and Hearst; when you didn't have anything to write about, you made it up.

The "Indian uprising" in Montana turned out to be the murder of one sheep rancher allegedly committed by three Cheyenne. Ac-cording to a detailed report from a government Indian agent in Tongue River and reported in the *Plain Dealer*, the three had been poaching sheep for food when the rancher came upon them. There was no mention in the newspaper story of the rancher shooting at the poachers, but it was a common practice. After the rancher was found dead with two bullet holes in him, Chief White Bull of the Cheyenne tribe was summoned to the Tongue River Indian Agency. There the government agent asked the chief to turn over to him the suspects involved in the shooting. The chief promised that if one of his braves was responsible for the murder, he would find him and turn him in. Weary and defeated, Indian leaders then often thought it better not to fight. When the chief told of his promise to an elder of the tribe, the old brave told his chief that he would turn in the murderer "if it is my own son." As it turned out, the elder's son was one of the poachers.

That same day of White Bull's meeting with the government official, a sheriff from nearby Custer County arrived at the Tongue River office with twenty-five newly minted deputies. The sheriff demanded the release of the suspects into his custody. What was reported in papers weeks earlier as marauding Indians turned out, according to the Indian agent, to be fellow tribe members protecting one of their own from what they perceived as a lynch mob. During the standoff, the cavalry showed up. White Bull hurriedly sent an emissary to the cavalry captain to assure him that the Cheyenne had no quarrel with U.S. solders. The three suspects were then turned over to the agent. The following day, after the soldiers had left, the Custer County sheriff returned, arrested the agent for violating state laws, and took custody of the three Cheyenne. The fate of the three Indians was not reported.

After escaping from Baltimore, the famous Cleveland Indian, Sockalexis, was to face his own judge and jury in the bleacher seats in a ballpark called the Polo Grounds. It was the biggest stage in baseball, and a place where Sockalexis would enjoy his finest moment. And the members of the press would gleefully skip back to their typewriters.

CLEVELANDS WIN THE GAME

They Hit Rusie Freely, and Played a Hustling, Aggressive, Winning Game.

SOCKALEXIS'S USUAL HOME RUN

Cincinnati, Philadelphia, Washington, Baltimore, and Boston Were the Other Winning Teams in Yesterday's League Games—Minor League Games.

How the Clubs Stand.

	Won.	Lost.	Per Cent.
Baltimore	32	9	.780
Boston	31	12	.721
Cincinnati	28	16	.619
New York	22	17	.564
Cleveland	22	20	.524
Philadelphia	24	22	.522
Brooklyn	22	21	.512
Pittsburg	20	22	.476
Louisville	17	26	.395
Chicago	17	27	.386
Washington	15	26	.366
St. Louis	8	38	.174

Results of Yesterday's Games.

At New York—Cleveland, 7; New York, 2.
At Brooklyn—Cincinnati, 15; Brooklyn, 6.
At Philadelphia—Philadelphia, 8; St. Louis, 7.
At Washington—Washington, 4; Louisville, 2.
At Baltimore—Baltimore, 10; Pittsburg, 5.
At Boston—Boston, 14; Chicago, 3.

To-day's Games.

Cleveland in New York.
Cincinnati in Brooklyn.
Pittsburg in Baltimore.
Louisville in Washington.
Chicago in Boston.
St. Louis in Philadelphia.

The Clevelands proved themselves quite a different proposition from the St. Louis men by easily defeating the New Yorks yesterday by the score of 7 to 2.

It is quite evident that Sockalexis, the Indian, whose phenomenal stick work has been one of the surprises of the season, has been giving the other Cleveland players some of his ideas as to how base hits

pitch to his credit. Hastings p[...] ly after the fourth, but the [...] been done. The playing of Da[...] nings was the feature. Score:

Baltimore	2	5	0	8	0
Pittsburg	0	0	2	0	0

Earned runs—Baltimore, 3. Ba[...] more, 11; Pittsburg, 6. Batter[...] Nops and Bowerman; Pittsburg, H[...] and Leahy. Errors—Baltimore, 2; Umpire—Mr. Hurst.

Boston, 14; Chicago

BOSTON, June 16.—The Chi[...] easy victims to-day, the Bosto[...] steady playing, piling up 14 ru[...] tors could not bat Nichols, an[...] fifth inning were as many as t[...] off him. Callahan would do[...] pitched a strong game had he[...] cent support. Kittredge's catc[...] redeeming feature of Chicago['...] batting of Stivetts, Collins, Lo[...] Nichols was the feature of the [...]

Boston	0	1	3	2	5
Chicago	0	0	0	1	1

Earned runs—Boston, 8. Base h[...] Chicago, 8. Batteries—Boston, N[...] gen; Chicago, Callahan and Kittr[...] Boston, 4; Chicago, 7. Umpire—M[...]

Brown, 13; Harvard

PROVIDENCE, R. I., June 1[...] feated Harvard in the closing [...] college season here to-day in a [...] was full of sensational featur[...] hitting and almost perfect fiel[...] game interesting. Brown led f[...] but Harvard gave the home [...] pull. The Brown team to-night [...] elected William Lauder, the [...] baseman, Captain for next yea[...]

Brown	3	1	0	4
Harvard	0	0	1	0

Batteries—Summersgill and Dun[...] and Scannell.

Indicted for Sunday Ba[...]

ROCHESTER, N. Y., June [...] ers and members of the Roch[...] Club will be arraigned in the [...] to-morrow on a charge of 8[...] ing. Indictments were foun[...] "Big Three," the name appl[...] Englert, Leimgruber, and Buc[...] ers of the team, and the [...] breaking the Sabbath on May [...] Indictments were found by t[...] that arose yesterday.

Manhattan, 11; Ford[...]

Manhattan College played t[...] with Fordham College on [...] grounds, at Fordham, yester[...] Fully 8,000 persons witness[...]

SUMMER 1897—*New York's governor, Frank S. Black, signs the Greater New York Charter, which will make Brooklyn part of New York City the following October. In June, George Tilyou opens Steeplechase Park in Coney Island with the words: "We Americans want to be thrilled or amused and we are ready to pay well for either sensation." During June, Columbia University continues its relocation from the East Side to Morningside Heights, taking over the grounds where the Bloomingdale Lunatic Asylum once stood. Chas. B. Lawlor and James W. Blake's 1894 tune "Sidewalks of New York" is still the most popular song in town. Arctic explorer Robert E. Peary arrives in New York on the steamship* Hope; *with him are six Eskimos from Greenland, including a seven-year-old boy named Minik. Some twenty thousand New Yorkers line up at the dock to pay twenty-five cents apiece to see the exotic visitors. Sometime later, the Eskimos are moved to the Museum of Natural History, where they are put on display. At night, when the museum closes, they sleep in the basement. Within months, four of the Eskimos, including Minik's father, die from tuberculosis. The fifth adult Eskimo then returns to Greenland, leaving Minik behind. Despite Minik's numerous attempts to retrieve them, his father's bones are kept by the museum for years. On June 15, the immigration buildings on Ellis Island are destroyed by fire.*

* * * *

AS THE GIANTS TOOK THE FIELD, the kinetic energy at the Polo Grounds turned to sound and built to a terrific drone. The noise was loudest down the left field line. There, hooligan Irish fans rose in unison with whiskeys or lagers in hand, in defiance of league rules. Copycatting John McGraw, more than a few wore Indian headdresses. The lot bellowed the now ubiquitous war whoop. The chant contagiously spread throughout the Polo Grounds until nearly the entire crowd was on its feet, the sound like ten thousand Apaches charging the circled wagons.

The scene, of course, startled Sockalexis. Not that he wasn't used to the abuse—Brooklyn and Boston were both fresh in his memory. But this was insane. It seemed to him that it was all leading up to this point: the newspapers with their Indian cartoons and "Chief Soc 'em"; the hooey about his father paddling the canoe to Washington, D.C.; McGraw and his war dance (the Baltimore third baseman should have prayed for rain, the Indian thought); an all-out-of-town run leading up to the big stage. New York. The Giants. As he stood in the dugout waiting his turn to bat, his gamer clutched in his hand, a small smile came to his face.

Seated in the stands behind the visitor's dugout, Frank Robison smiled too. The magnate was on the National League owners committee that had, the prior winter, hammered out a deal where gates would be shared fifty-fifty between the home and visiting teams. The idea was to keep struggling franchises like Pittsburgh and

Louisville financially solvent. But hell, he was having his own money problems. How could he possibly run a successful baseball franchise without Sunday gates? "An absolute day of rest," the clergy had said to the *Plain Dealer*. "If Sunday is to be an absolute day of rest, why should the churches be opened on that day?" the magnate shot back. The quote had got him in hot water with some of the Euclid Avenue crowd, a position that he lately found himself in with alarming frequency. The hell with them, he thought, as he sat back contentedly on his seat. Those phonies didn't go to games anyhow. They certainly didn't ride his streetcars. Cleveland was a working-class town, for God's sake. His crowd had gnarly hands and coal dust caked behind their ears. Ah, but those problems were six hundred miles away. As he patted his thick middle, he gazed at the wonderful bedlam around him.

The double-tiered, horseshoe-shaped grandstand, the first of what would become the standard for big league ballparks, was packed with cranks. As were the bleachers that extended from the grandstand and enclosed the entire field. Even the center field bleachers, five hundred feet from home plate, in front of the rise where the rich businessmen and the Park Avenue types sat in carriages to take in a few innings, were filled to capacity. The sight was a familiar one to Robison. Over the first months of the season, in cities like St. Louis and Cincinnati, the parks were also filled. Signing the Indian, he would say, was the best move he ever made. Better even than luring the boy they called the Cyclone from the farm.

The weather had cooperated. After the miserable conditions in Brooklyn, Boston, and Washington, the rainy front had finally slid off the coast and over the Atlantic. Above Coogan's Bluff, the sky was a dome of robin's-egg blue with just a few puffy clouds motoring slowly by in the faint breeze. The matchup was perfect too. That Amos Rusie was on the mound for the Giants was almost enough to fill the park. After a tough start and rust from a year's absence, Rusie had begun to round into form. Nobody in the league threw harder, and he owned a fast, nasty curveball that turned even the best hitter's front leg into marmalade. Hell, the Waldorf Hotel didn't name a cocktail after just anybody. Sockalexis had hit him hard in Cleveland, but it wasn't the same Rusie on the mound this day. If the pop the ball made when it hit Jack Warner's catcher's mitt during his warm-up was any indication, the whole Cleveland team was in for a long afternoon.

Still, Robison had faith in his team. Though the eastern swing hadn't been kind, there was still a lot of baseball to be played. Patsy Tebeau had promised him that the team was just going through some hard luck and bad bounces. Robison wondered how many bad bounces could add up to the twenty-one runs the Beaneaters had scored on the Indians in Boston. But the team looked good against Washington. Hell, the magnate thought as he smiled, Tebeau knew what he was doing. In Robison's estimation, Tebeau was the best baseball man in the land.

The magnate's mood soured as he looked across the field and saw Freedman sitting behind the Giants dugout. Robison wasn't one to meddle in how others ran their teams, unless of course they cost him money. And Freedman had done just that.

Perhaps there has never been a man in the annals of baseball so universally disliked as Andrew Freedman. His obituary in the *Sporting News* read, in part: "He had an arbitrary disposition, a violent temper, and an ungovernable tongue in anger which was easily provoked and he was disposed to be arbitrary to the point of tyranny with subordinates." And that publication was kind. Freedman's association with the Giants began in January of 1895. He used his Tammany Hall connections and acumen as a scoundrel real-estate lawyer to obtain controlling interest in the team. He bought his first shares of the team in a client's name. There was only one small problem with the transaction: He hadn't let the client know. Fittingly, in the circuslike atmosphere the Giants would assume under Freedman, the client was James A. Bailey, who later would join forces with P. T. Barnum. In 1895, Freedman swindled the rest of the Giants shares out of Edward Talcott, paying about a quarter of what Talcott's stock was worth.

Once Freedman held the reins of the team, the insanity began. À la early George Steinbrenner, he hired and fired managers with wanton indifference, including future Hall of Famer and baseball visionary John Montgomery Ward. That move would come back to haunt him. Undoubtedly his most bizarre choice of manager was Harvey Watkins, an actor with no prior baseball experience. But then again, perhaps Watkins's previous job made him a model employee under Freedman's reign—he had worked in James Bailey's circus.

If Freedman had anyone in New York on his side, and it's doubtful that he did, he lost their favor in his dispute with Amos Rusie. The pitcher was about as well liked as a player could be. Tall, strapping, and single, Rusie often kept company with Broadway starlets. Weber and Fields, a popular vaudeville team of the time, did a skit in his honor. But what endeared him to New York fans was the way he could pitch. In six seasons with the Giants, Rusie had won an astounding 179 games. At just twenty-four years old, he had a future as bright as a summer morning on the Indiana farm were he was born.

After the 1895 season, one in which Rusie won twenty-three games, Freedman fined him two hundred dollars for missing curfew. It was a not too subtly veiled attempt to cut payroll. Rusie refused to pay the fine, and when Freedman sent a contract for the 1896 season, minus the two hundred dollars, Rusie wouldn't sign it. Although the press and fans were calling for Freedman's blood, the Giants owner refused to back down. In turn, Rusie refused to pay it. In protest, the "Hoosier Thunderbolt" sat out the entire 1896 season. It was then he retained the services of a lawyer—one John Montgomery Ward.

As he sat in the stands, Robison remembered Freedman calling Rusie "a dumb farm boy." Yeah, he was dumb all right, Robison mused, dumb enough to hire the one guy on the whole planet who would strike fear in every National League team owner. The thought of Ward and his 1891 player revolt had the league board falling over one another to rule in Rusie's favor. Still, the "stubborn sheeny," as his own player, James "Ducky" Holmes, would later call Freedman, wouldn't give in. He told the New York papers, "The New York club will not be party to any conciliatory step." Finally, every single other magnate had to pony up the dough, eventually paying the fine, Rusie's salary for 1896, and even the raise in pay the pitcher demanded to play in 1897. Even after all of that, the blockhead Freedman told his manager, Bill Joyce, not to let Rusie pitch. Only after catching hell from the cranks, editorials in the New York papers screaming for his neck, and a six-game losing streak in April did Freedman give in and let Joyce play his star pitcher. But that was past history. Today, as Robison was fond of saying, is money.

Sockalexis was batting third. Up until this day, Tebeau had him in the leadoff slot to take advantage of his speed. It seemed he could steal bases at will; he stole most of them standing up. With Cupid Childs hitting about .350, and with Crab Burkett, just about the best hitter in the league, behind him, Tebeau saw an RBI opportunity every time Sock could work a base on balls—more than once that season the Indian had scored from first on a single. But on the road trip Sock was hitting the ball too hard to waste him batting first. Even during the oh-fer he took in Boston, he was smacking the ball; it was just his rotten luck that he was hitting it right into their leather. Anyway, if he hit the ball like he did in Washington, there isn't a leather in the world going to catch it—it was one of the longest home runs Tebeau had ever seen. Besides, why not put the Indian in the marquis spot? That's what these lushed-up Micks in the crowd paid their two bits to see.

In the dugout, Sockalexis had to smile. This was the rowdiest crowd yet. In some ways he was comfortable with his celebrity. Lately he took to doffing his cap at the howling cranks, as if to say, *Scream all the nonsense you want, I know I'm the one you came to see and I'm gonna give you your money's worth.* Stereotypically, the sportswriters called him "brooding" and "stoic." He might have been stoic at the plate—still as a totem pole as he pressed the handle of the bat to his heart, the only movement the gentle sway of the barrel, like a lake reed in a summer breeze. But that intensity would melt with his smile, the coal-black eyes pressed to glimmering diamonds.

When Sockalexis smiled, and he smiled often, that stern concentration unfolded into pure magnetism that worked like catnip on the ladies and was pure gold for Robison. The first story about his female following had appeared in the *Sporting News*. The writer called them "Soc's pale-faced maidens." At League Park, Ladies Day drew twice as many this year as it did last year. And it wasn't only in Cleveland. There were young girls with placards in Chicago, and in Cincinnati they took to wearing single feathers like Indian squaws. But Robison knew this display of affection didn't sit well with everyone. No doubt it was a heated topic of discussion among those stuffy churchwomen. But Sock wasn't dumb. He knew not to be seen publicly in the company of a white woman; it wasn't too long ago that they hung Indians for that. The other players in the league would probably beat him with baseball bats. What did that blockhead Delahanty say about the Indian? "The league has gone all to hell now that they're letting them damn foreigners in." He wouldn't know an Indian from a fence post.

But Robison wasn't worried about Sockalexis satisfying his natural urges. Cleveland had enough houses of ill repute to keep him off the street and out of trouble for a couple of seasons at least. Robison did keep an eye on the Indian's drinking. Tebeau had told the magnate that he had a tight leash on the rookie, but Robison wasn't so sure. Word had gotten back that Sockalexis spent just about every evening in the downtown saloons. He liked the attention he received. Just two months in the league and the rookie was the biggest thing in Cleveland. When he walked into the barroom, the fair-weather crowd lined up to buy him drinks. It wasn't the best of crowds, either: fast talkers and sharpies. Sock had even taken to dressing like them. No Sears & Roebuck catalogue suits for him. Even had one suit made by a haberdasher in New York and sent all the way to Cleveland. With the money Sockalexis was spending on clothing, booze, and ladies of the evening, his season's salary would be gone before the Fourth of July. Robison didn't have a problem with the Indian having his fun. Just as long as he showed up sober for the games.

The umpire signaled the game to start, and Crab Burkett strode to the plate. The fans stood and stomped the wooden bleachers, the sound a daunting rhythmic thunder. The noise was especially loud in the left field bleachers. That section of the Polo Grounds was called "Burkville," and you had to have a name that started with *Mc* or *O'* or have the map of the County Cork on your face to sit there. The fights were legendary in Burkville, sometimes more entertaining than the game. And the police were no help. Most of the New York cops had family in that section.

As he stepped to the plate, the Irish contingent turned its ire on Burkett. *Let one of them come over the fence,* Burkett thought, *and I'll give 'em the same treatment I gave to the joker in Cleveland.* The fan had rushed onto the field at League Park and took a swing at the center fielder. Burkett then belted him over the head with his bat. The fan left the park in an ambulance.

In the batter's box, he dug in and glared out at Rusie. The big right-hander stared back. At the peak of his Hall of Fame career Burkett was one of the toughest outs in the league, but there was more here than just athletic competition. The two had history. In a league filled with ornery players, Burkett took the cup. He hated everybody: fans, umpires, owners, opposing players, and even some members of his own team. His choice of language would make a felon blush. As is frequently the case with such hotheads, he was also easily taunted. One of the favorite ways players got under the Crab's skin was to call him "Pebbly" Glasscock, to whom Burkett owned a slight resemblance. Pebbly, an old-time shortstop for Cleveland and Cincinnati, had garnered his moniker because of his habit of groundskeeping his position—picking up pebbles and tossing them aside. It has been said that most of the time the pebbles were imaginary. Also, Pebbly was not the best-looking fellow in the world. He had ears like two open doors on a taxicab. In 1889, Glasscock managed a minor league team in Indiana. There he discovered the Hoosier Thunderbolt and was responsible for the righty's entrance into the big leagues. When Rusie faced Burkett, he would yell "Pebbly Junior!" Burkett's neck would get red and, more often than not, he would swing so hard at the pitch that he'd nearly screw himself into the ground.

But this day Rusie needed no such help. He made quick work of Burkett, striking the left fielder out on three straight pitches— three knuckle-breaking curveballs, a pitch that today would be called a slider and owned by Roger Clemens, a pitch that when he had it working made Rusie virtually unhittable. The crowd sensed this, and as Childs followed Burkett to the plate, their cheers gained momentum.

Childs was no easy out either. As a kind of reminder of who was in charge, Rusie ran a fastball up and in, knocking Childs to the dirt. The crowd let out a collective "ooohhh," like the sound of steam escaping. Childs jumped back up, brushed himself off, and determinedly took his stance. The next pitch gave the appearance of coming right down the middle of the plate, but at the last second it dove low and away. All Childs could do was wave at it. Rusie smiled. Today, he could do whatever he wanted, and what he wanted was the Indian. The quote was printed in most of the New York papers and picked up in Cleveland by the *Plain Dealer*.

Rusie had vowed to fan the Indian. The pitcher didn't particularly like the way Sockalexis had feasted on him in Cleveland, and he surely didn't like all the ink the rookie was getting. Rusie was a star of the first order. He had paid his dues for seven seasons, one of those years for the current lunatic owner of the Giants. Who the hell was this rookie to be getting all the attention? On the third pitch, Childs swung as hard as he could and drilled the ball straight into the Polo Grounds earth in front of the plate. Catcher Warner pounced on it and lobbed it to first. Two outs. The anticipation in the crowd was electric.

Sockalexis had watched every pitch with rapt concentration. In his mind's eye he timed the last-second break of Rusie's curveball. In his heart he knew he could hit it. The Indian walked to the plate with the bat on his shoulder. Although it didn't seem possible, the noise grew even louder, the stamping of feet a cadence to the bedlam. Sock dug his back foot into the rut in the batter's box. Warner dropped his hand between his knees and flashed the signs. There was no need. Everybody in the park knew what Rusie was going to throw. The Indian was going to get his best—the hardest curve in baseball.

Sensing the moment, the crowd stilled. Savvy as they were, they knew something special might happen. In the stillness, the Indian heard a familiar sound. It came from down the left field line, from Burkville. Members of his tribe had come all the way from Maine to cheer him on and had sat right in the middle of the Irish mob to do so. Later he would find out that his father was among them.

Rusie toed the hard board on the mound and swung into his windup, both hands reaching toward the sky. Sockalexis was perfectly still. For a moment, time froze—then the ball was hurtling toward the plate. The Indian stepped into the pitch.

Only in hindsight does one know when the penultimate moment in his life occurs. In the exuberance of youth, on that long New York summer's day, a day he thought would last forever—when he could laugh off a drunken night, when he was bulletproof and his legs would forever carry him swiftly—in those wonderful slow-motion seconds the Indian had no way of knowing that this was his defining moment. As the bat made contact, he felt almost no vibration in his hands; for a batter, the sweetest sensation in the world is hearing the crack but feeling nothing. The ball creased the blue sky like a midday comet, sailing over the right field bleachers and bouncing down the 8th Avenue steps of the Polo Grounds. No one—none of the players, none of the cranks—had ever seen a ball land there, and for a moment, as if catching its collective breath, the crowd was silent.

As Sockalexis cantered toward first, his head modestly down, his legs carrying him on air, a peculiar thing happened. In a gracious, almost polite manner, the cranks, still on their feet, began to applaud. The working-class Irish fans—they who had suffered their own indignities, those who had been the most brutal toward the Indian—were doffing their caps. In baseball, the great equalizer of men at its purest, it was how you played, not where you came from.

As Sock rounded third and passed by Burkville, he allowed himself a smile and a nod to his family and childhood friends. He caught a glimpse of his father and the proud expression on the old man's face.

In a better seat, Robison's smile turned to an ear-swallowing grin. Though it would be three months later that the famous letter to the editor would appear in the *New York Sun*, Robison could have written the reply right then: "Yes, Virginia, there is a Santa Claus."

BLOOD POISONING.

That is Outfielder Sock-alexis' Latest Af-fliction.

He is Taken to a Hospital.

are May Save Him Serious Trouble, but Amputation May Possibly be Necessary—A New Kick on the L. A. W.—The C. W. C.'s Coming Race and Outing—Beckwith Knocks Out His Man—Other Sporting.

YESTERDAY'S RESULTS.

Pittsburg .... 3—Louisville 2
Baltimore ....14—Brooklyn 5
Boston ...... 5—Washington ... 2
New York .... 7—Philadelphia ... 2

The Standing.

Clubs.	W.	L.	Pr.Ct.
Boston	65	30	685
Baltimore	61	30	670
Cincinnati	59	32	648
New York	55	36	604
Cleveland	50	44	532
Chicago	47	51	480
Pittsburg	43	51	457
Louisville	43	55	439
Philadelphia	42	54	438
Brooklyn	38	55	409
Washington	37	56	398
St. Louis	26	72	265

Games Today.

Brooklyn at Baltimore.
Washington at Boston.
Philadelphia at New York.

Sockalexis, Cleveland's erstwhile famous outfielder; the Indian who caused such a furore in the baseball world, did not leave on the eastern trip with the Cleveland team—In fact he will be a pretty lucky In-

Clingman, 3b.. ..... 4 0 3
Wilson, c.. .... 3 0 1
Cunningham, p.... .. 4 0 0

Totals 35 2 12
Pittsburg 0 0 0 0 0 0
Louisville 2 0 0 0 0 0

Earned runs—Pittsburg 3, Lou
Two-base hits—Padden, Clingman
base hits—Davis, Clark. Sacrif
Padden, Wagner, Wilson. Stole
Clark. Double plays—Ely to P
Rothfuss; Stafford to Dolan to
First base on balls—Off Gardn
Cunningham 1. Struck out—By
5, by Cunningham 2. Left on bas
burg 6, Louisville 10. First
errors—Pittsburg 1. Time—1:3
pire—McDonald.

Baltimore 14—Brooklyn

BALTIMORE, Aug. 16.—The O
day defeated the Brooklyns in a
game. Kennedy held the champi
to two hits during the first four
but in the fifth a succession of w
hits netted the home team five
the next inning the visitors becan
alized and for the remainder of
there was no contest. Attendan
Score:

Baltimore.	A.B.	R.	H.
Keeler, r. f.	5	3	2
Jennings, s. s.	2	3	1
Kelley, l. f.	5	2	4
Stenzel, c. f.	5	2	2
Doyle, 1b	5	1	1
Reitz, 2b	4	1	1
Quinn, 3b	5	1	2
Clark, c.	5	0	1
Pond, p.	5	1	0
Totals	41	14	14

Brooklyn.	A.B.	R.	H.
Jones, r. f.	4	1	3
Griffin, c. f.	5	0	0
Shindle, 3b	5	0	0
Anderson, 1b	4	2	1
A. Smith, l. f.	4	0	1
Shoch, 2b	2	1	2
Burrell, c.	4	1	1
Kennedy, p.	4	0	0
G. Smith, s. s.	4	0	2
Totals	36	5	10

Baltimore 1 0 1 0 5 6 1
Brooklyn . ..2 0 0 0 0 3 0

Earned runs—Baltimore 4, B
Two-base hits—Anderson, Stenz
Three-base hit—Jones. Home
rell. Stolen bases—Jennings 2,
Jones, Keeler, Shoch, Anderson

9

SUMMER 1897—*According to the* Cleveland Plain Dealer, *on August 14 a Choctaw Indian sentenced to die for the murder of a fellow tribesman is granted a stay of execution to play in a big baseball game. The governor of the Choctaw tribe there is a baseball fan, and the condemned Indian, Wah Teh Nish, is the star of the governor's favorite team; he was supposed to be shot on the day of the game, but the execution is postponed for two days so he can be in the lineup. In July, coal strikes dominate the front page of newspapers across the country. Slowly but surely, the button is being fazed out in the production of men's trousers, replaced by Whitcomb L. Judson's invention: the zipper. On July 9 the entire city of Cleveland is equipped with street signs. Alexander Winton, a former bicycle manufacturer on Cleveland's west side, is a common sight on city streets in the six-cylinder automobile he developed; he is also a common sight sprawled on the street, having been bucked from his auto. Winton would go on to design the steering mechanisms and braking systems that Henry Ford would utilize in his mass-produced cars.*

* * * *

BY JULY, SOCKALEXIS WAS SOAKING UP the nightlife in Cleveland like a dry rag on a wet bar. Dressed in English tweed, with a Cuban cigar lodged in the corner of his mouth, he was a regular sight in city saloons. The *Cleveland Plain Dealer* took notice and began to warn the rookie star about his bright-light carousing: "Other players have imagined they could keep pace with fast ball playing company in the daytime and fast company in general all night, but something generally occurs to change their mind in this particular." But the loneliness of instant stardom and racial difference combined with the temptations of the Cleveland night was like an ocean to a man dying of thirst. Like most of the burgeoning metropolises in America then, Cleveland had more than its share of salt water.

Named after the Third Police District that patrolled the area, the Roaring Third was then Cleveland's center of drinking, gambling, and prostitution. Saloons regularly disregarded closing laws and stayed open all night. Once fashionable, Short Vincent, an abbreviated block behind the Hollenden Hotel, had also degenerated. Prostitutes and assorted characters worked the block. One named "Kelly the Piper" would for the price of a beer play a tune on his bagpipes. The section east of Erie Street was the Tenderloin, where prostitutes worked openly with little hindrance from authorities and common citizens alike. Prostitution also flourished in a section bounded by Ontario, Lakeside, Superior, and East 12th Streets. Abandoned mansions, once owned by wealthy Clevelanders, now housed brothels that operated with almost complete impunity. Like clockwork, once a month the Cleveland Police Department would raid the establishments, but these sorties were likely collection runs and opportunities for the ranking partici- pants to enjoy free samples of the house's wares. To any single young man first visiting Cleveland, the gay sounds of the bawdy saloons were a welcome comfort; the red lights of the Tenderloin shone like friendly beacons. For Sockalexis, it was about as friendly as a shark tank.

In the July 22 edition of the *Plain Dealer*, baseball fans read again of the Indian's drinking problem:

> It is no longer a secret that the local management can no longer control Sockalexis, and when that management once loses control of a player it is likely to be "all off" between said management and said player. This is an unfortunate fact for the team and also for Sockalexis. When the Indian came here he was ambitious and his head was level. He was courted by a pretty lively crowd and then the trouble began. Discipline had no effect. When a player begins to realize that he is the whole thing nothing can stop him.
>
> Manager Tebeau still has hopes that the great Indian will come to his senses. . . . If Sockalexis takes proper care of himself his baseball career is bound to be a most brilliant one. If not, he will soon find that he was a nine-day wonder and that the nine days have passed. It will not take many days to decide the fate of Cleve- land's great find.

Sock's season began to unravel on the Fourth of July. There are sev- eral variations of what happened that night. Some time after

159

Sockalexis had left professional baseball, Tebeau told a reporter his version:

> He celebrated the 4th of July by an all-night carousal in a red light
> joint, during which he jumped out a second-story window. His
> right foot was badly broken in the fall, but he bandaged it up and
> went with the other players to Pittsburgh that night. I went over
> the next day and hurried out to Exposition Park and there in the
> bus was Soc, his broken foot swollen four or five times its natural
> size. I sent him back to Cleveland, where a doctor put his foot in
> a plaster cast and ordered him not to even turn over in bed.
>
> But do you know, he would get up during the night and walk
> a block on his plaster foot to get a drink of whiskey.

Some newspaper reports at the time intimate that Sockalexis had jumped from the window to escape detectives or team officials who had been following his antics. It was common practice for teams then to hire detectives to keep an eye on the more rambunctious players. Out of control drinking was so rampant in the league, however, that once a detective reported a player excessively drinking, the manager of the team was left with the question of how to punish them. Suspensions were rare. Popular players were too valuable as drawing cards to sit out games, and firing a player of such stature was just not done. An example of baseball management's predicament ran in the *Chicago Post*:

"Woe is me." That is Stallings' cry, echoed about Philadelphia today and sent over the telegraph wires. Four of the best men on the manager's team are in disgrace. Detectives have reported that they have taken to drink to such an extent that they cannot play ball. Stallings is in a quandary. He dare not release them outright for they would be gobbled up so quickly that the city of brotherly love would be blinded by the meteoric flash of contracts, and he knows not how to punish them.

It is not far-fetched at all to believe that the Indian did in fact injure himself to escape detectives. Yet baseball's oral narrators have a way of sidestepping defaming stories. Years after the Sock's death, Burkett told a reporter that the Indian injured himself chasing down a runaway baby carriage.

It was also common knowledge that Sockalexis often kept company with fast women who made their living out of the saloons on Short Vincent and frequently patronized Cleveland's houses of ill repute. There is good reason why he found comfort in prostitutes: There was nowhere else for him to go. Though lady fans had crowded ballparks around the country to watch his muscular form, there was the greatest of distances between this voyeuristic fantasy and a real physical relationship. For a white lady to keep public company with an Indian was about as common as an out-in-the-open black and white coupling. Though circumstance was undoubtedly stacked against him, it was Sockalexis's drinking that was the root of all his problems, and no amount of advice from newspapers or any other source could stem the downward spiral of his addiction.

"No other player to my knowledge ever sacrificed so much on the altar of his appetite than did this red man," Tebeau was once quoted as saying. "When he began to drink and stay out all night, I promised him $6000 for the next season and $10,000 for 1899 if he would stay sober and play ball."

This might have been a slight exaggeration on Tebeau's part. No player then in the league made six thousand dollars, let alone ten thousand dollars. In those years, well before baseball clubs were valued in the hundreds of millions of dollars, many clubs struggled just to make payroll, never mind a profit, and with Sunday baseball banned, Cleveland was one of these struggling franchises. Still, Tebeau's story gives insight, albeit hindsight, to just how valuable Sockalexis was to the Cleveland team.

The "official" story reported in the *Plain Dealer* was that the Indian was scratched from the lineup because of a "sore foot." Somehow Sockalexis managed to get into games on July 9 and 11 and even went four-for-nine over the two games. It seems incredible that he could play at all on a severely broken foot, but even if it were just a slight fracture or badly sprained, he was clearly not the same player. On July 13 the *Plain Dealer* ran the headline "Wooden Indian" to describe the right fielder's play, chiding him that a "good night's rest" was all he needed. He would be afforded the opportunity. His name would not be in the lineup card next until July 25.

Sock's job was clearly in jeopardy. Though in the papers Tebeau offered a tepid vote of confidence, he was actively looking for a replacement. Earlier in July, Jimmy McAleer had left the team after an extended batting slump that had prompted criticism from Tebeau. Several times in the past, McAleer's dry spells had incited the manager's ire, but each time the two were able to patch things up. This time, however, McAleer cleaned out his locker and left town before the manager had a chance to mollify him. With the Indian crisis leaving his outfield in shambles, Tebeau wired McAleer and begged him to return. McAleer played hard to get. Returning to Cleveland to take in a day at the races, McAleer told a reporter that he had "no intentions of returning to the game this year at least."

In the meantime, Tebeau fashioned a patchwork outfield, shuttling Lewis "Sport" McAllister, a second-year player known more for his glove work than his batting skill, and Jack O'Connor, a grisly old veteran who was reliable at the plate but a liability in the field. Despite all the furor, the Indians were playing fairly well, ten games over .500, placing them in the middle of the first division, just two games behind New York and only four behind their hated rival, Baltimore. Though the streaking Beaneaters were eleven games up, with more than two months left in the season Cleveland was still a contender.

On the eve of his return to the lineup, the *Plain Dealer* again lectured Sock: "Many a young ball player has gone through Sockalexis' recent difficulties successfully and finally got down to good, conscientious work. A successful young player is very apt to imagine that he will revolutionize the league, but he usually gets over the notion if he holds his job long enough." The article hinted that Sockalexis had grown distasteful of the recent chiding by sportswriters: "Threats to exterminate the race of sporting writers do not frighten anybody, and unlimited ability as a pugilist does not make a man one whit the better ball player."

On his return to the diamond, Sockalexis showed why management was giving him a long leash. He hit the ball hard in all three of his at bats. Two of them would have gone easily for extra bases but, hobbled as he was, Sock had thought better than to chance being thrown out at second. In the field his handicap proved even more pronounced. He struggled to reach a lazy pop hit by Ed Delahanty, and then he let the ball drop out of his mitt. When he finally recovered he threw wild to the plate, allowing at least one run to score. The muff was a sign of worse fielding to come.

Sockalexis no longer owned his greatest attribute—his speed. The outcome of the game, however, was decided not on the Indian's good or bad play, or, for that matter, on anyone's play. A last-minute substitute umpire was officiating the game and from the first pitch he was abused by the visiting Philadelphia club. The profanation grew to a point that the ump finally had enough and forfeited the game to Cleveland. The score, 9–0 in favor of the Indians, went into the record books.

Robison had won his most recent battle for Sunday baseball. A local judge ruled that the Sunday ban was unconstitutional, and he granted a stay until a court date in September. If Robison wanted a show of public support, he got it. Nearly fifteen thousand cranks filled the stands in League Park, spilling out onto foul territory of the field. Robison's greed matched the size of the crowd. The magnate had the outfield fences removed so as to fit every last crank with four bits through his turnstiles.

When the Indian came to the plate in the first inning, he was met with a huge response from the crowd. Not all of it was positive. From the stands, comments and jeers about his drinking and carousing cascaded to right field. Reminiscent of Sock's debut in New York, there were also the hauntingly familiar intonations of the Penobscot language. Whether the appearance that day of the Indian's fellow tribesmen and family was just coincidental, or whether it was Robison's not-so-subtle attempt to settle his prized possession down, would be conjecture. What is documented is how Sockalexis responded to their presence.

If the fences had remained in place, the high, arching drive would have certainly been a home run. As it was, the ball scattered the thick crowd beyond Wee Willie Keeler, the Orioles' right fielder. By the time Keeler rooted the ball from the tangle of fans' feet, the big Indian had limped in for a stand-up triple. Again, like that day in New York, the mixed reception he had first received turned unanimously to a solid wall of cheers. Sock doffed his cap at the adoring crowd. Absolved of his transgressions at least for the moment, he had won them back with a simple flick of his bat.

Five days later, on July 31, Sockalexis was suspended from the Indians and did not accompany the team on its trip to Cincinnati. If there was any doubt—and there was very little—that he had a drinking problem, it was erased during those five days. He didn't draw a sober breath during that span. Only when he passed out did the drinking stop, just to start again when he came to. Cleveland at the end of July was blisteringly hot. On awakening, the Indian shook violently from dehydration and sweated profusely from alcohol poisoning and unbearable temperatures.

Though this was years before such terms were coined, Sockalexis was exhibiting textbook alcoholism, complete with feelings of low self-esteem and self-worth, and in the insidiousness of the disease he was blowing the one thing where he drew both. One can only imagine what demons lurked in his hangover-addled thoughts: *You are a screwup, a drunk, a good-for-nothing.* It was a horse race as to which felt worse, those imagined voices or the physical pain. He had no choice; there was only one thing that would alleviate both: the bottle. He would pick it up again. He had to.

Under the headline "A Broken Idol," the *Plain Dealer* ran this story:

Sockalexis, Cleveland's sensational right fielder is on the ragged edge. He did not go to Cincinnati with the team for reasons now apparent. President Robison began an investigation recently and yesterday the result was made known to Mr. Sockalexis. The result was that for four sprees within the past few days the Indian must settle. For the first offense he is fined $20. For the second $50. For the third $100 and for the fourth he is suspended without pay. The suspension will not be raised, says Mr. Robison, until the Indian is in fit condition to play ball and until he makes affidavit that he will sip no more intoxicants until the baseball season is over.

This action will not be a surprise to many who have observed the Indian carefully, and the only wonder is that he did not get into trouble with the management of the club before this.

Even in an era rife with drunkenness, and even considering a double standard, Sockalexis's drinking stood out and caused a furor among his teammates. Several players had grumbled to Tebeau about his performance. The team's reaction was surely a trait unique to the American sons of immigrants, that unlikely mixture of Calvinism and inebriation where one could get as boxed as one would like as long as one showed up for work the next day. The Indian was breaking the cardinal rule, and his Irish-American and German-American teammates weren't having it. So unnerved was Robison about the mental state of his team that he fired off a volley of telegrams to Tebeau in first Cincinnati and later Louisville demanding updates on their condition. Tebeau, with the comfort of distance, had wired back: "Everyone is trying to win, disappointed but not discouraged."

But the truth was, the team was coming apart. In Cincinnati the Indian's replacement, O'Connor, went missing on an apparent bender. On a scheduled day off, Tebeau took a train to Fort Wayne, Indiana, where he signed minor league outfielder Fred Cook to a season contract. The manager was not expecting the Indian's return and he was trying to fill the huge void left by his absence. Still, Tebeau seemed to be holding on to Sockalexis by the thinnest of threads. A home game scheduled against the Giants was postponed because of a "wet" League Park. Sportswriters wondered if the manager had sanctioned the postponement in order to give Sock time to get himself together. Of course, while Tebeau was stalling for time, team detectives were charging for their time watching the Indian's performance in local saloons.

For all of the histrionics, Sock might not have been suspended had he not cost Robison in the pocketbook. Tebeau had to buy Cook from the Fort Wayne team, a price that undoubtedly was dear. The outfielder was the captain, manager, and somewhat of a local hero of the minor league team. Along with buying out his contract, Robison had to pay him for the year. As it turned out, it was not the wisest of investments. Cook played in a total of five games for Cleveland and never again played in the big leagues.

Sockalexis served out his suspension and returned to the team lineup on August 14. The Friday afternoon crowd at League Park welcomed him back with a hearty ovation, but this time he could not feed off the crowd's enthusiasm. He looked gaunt and anemic. He was a paltry one-for-four at the plate, with the only hit a slow infield roller that was muffed by the fielder. The Indians managed to eek out a 6–5 victory and take the season series from St. Louis, but at eighteen games behind Boston, Cleveland was playing out the string. Meanwhile, Sockalexis was hanging from one.

Two days later, Sock had a brush with death. As the team readied for an eastern road trip, the Indian was rushed to Huron Street Hospital for what the *Plain Dealer* reported as blood poisoning. "Sockalexis, Cleveland's erstwhile famous outfielder; the Indian who caused such a furor in the baseball world, did not leave on the eastern trip with the Cleveland team—in fact he will be a pretty lucky Indian if he plays ball again this season, and there is a chance that he will never be seen on the diamond again." The article went on to state that the Indian had contracted the disease neglecting his broken foot, and, in its overly dire tone, suggested amputation as a possibility.

At the hospital, Robison visited his once-prized possession. There he both chastised and coddled the Indian. The magnate assured him that he would be kept on the team's payroll while he recuperated, but only if he again swore off the booze. Doctors at the hospital told Sockalexis and Robison that, in the *Plain Dealer*'s words, "the serious results were brought on by dissipation." His foot was irreparably damaged as a result of the jump from the brothel window and the lack of care, but it was only one of his physical problems. Later the Indian would deny that he in fact had blood poisoning. According to the *Louisville Courier-Journal*, Sockalexis sent a letter to a Holy Cross teammate to say his condition wasn't as bad as reported in newspapers. He promised his old mate that he would "get back into the game and show the public his old-time form." The most likely explanation of the hospital stay is that the team had orchestrated it as nothing other than a forced detoxification.

By the 1890s the history of treatment of alcoholics in this country was a slowly developing story marked with minor successes and a great deal of ignorance. It would be after Prohibition that the medical community began seriously considering alcoholism as a disease. Perhaps the first physician to embrace the then-radical disease theory was Dr. Benjamin Rush. In 1784, Rush published a pamphlet called "Inquiry into the Effects of Spiritous Liquors on the Human Body and Mind." In the pamphlet was a graph that charted the effects of escalating levels of consumption. For example, drinking too much brandy and grog led to inflamed eyes, a red nose, fighting, a predilection for horse racing, and finally black eyes and rags. The pamphlet listed diseases that stemmed from alcoholism, including fetid breath, frequent and disgusting belching, jaundice, and dropping of belly and limbs. Though Rush believed fermented beverages—beer and wine—to be beneficial to health, he also believed distilled spirits to be habit forming with an end result, for those predisposed to the disease, of complete physical and moral breakdown. According to Rush, madness patiently awaited the alcoholic.

In was in the early 1800s when the temperance movement

started, and with it the first link between religion and the treatment of alcoholism. Fueled by Protestant oratory, the temperance movement rapidly spread throughout the country and remained a religious and political force until the repeal of the Eighteenth Amendment. One of the more quixotic temperance groups was the Washingtonians. Inspired by a minister's sermon, six self-described drunken customers of the Chase Tavern in Baltimore decided to swear off the bottle. They formed group meetings, a precursor to Alcoholics Anonymous. Invoking the legendary honesty of our first president, each member would take turns describing the horrors of their drinking lives. Also like AA, they sought to spread the message, and for a while were wildly successful in doing so. The Washingtonians, however, were a loosely knit organization, and they disappeared just as quickly as they had come into vogue.

Undoubtedly the most politically powerful offshoot of the temperance movement was the Anti-Saloon League. Though in the beginning the temperance movement was primarily nonpolitical, a growing number of people believed that the solution to America's alcohol problem was legislation. The Anti-Saloon League began in Oberlin, Ohio, and, with the backing of the Protestant ministry, quickly became one of the state's most influential lobbies. Candidates for local and state office were elected on planks of working toward complete abstention. By 1896 the organization was one of the most powerful political machines in the country.

But for the chronic alcoholic of the 1890s, the political growth and machinations of the temperance movement mattered little.

Their solution to alcoholism was to forcibly keep the drunk from the bottle, a tactic that in practice had little hope of succeeding.

If there was a moment of clarity as the Indian tossed and turned with night sweats, he might have realized his season was over. It's a stretch, however, to assume he then had the forethought to see that he was being ushered out of the stage door of celebrity, that the same newspapermen who wrote in such flattering terms of his talent would turn sarcastic and derisive, that he would never again be the player that flamed through the league—that his life was heading on an inexorable march to despair and ruin. That stark reality, like the coming of a cold Maine winter, would be on him before he knew it.

On August 4 the *New York Times* reported that Sockalexis was about to be released from the Cleveland club. Ollie Pickering, an outfielder released earlier that season from Louisville, was to be picked up. Though Pickering did join the team, Tebeau held out hope that the Indian could straighten out, and he kept the rookie on the roster. On August 24 the *Washington Post* gave its readers an update on the Sockalexis saga: "Oliver Patruccio Tebeau, the leader of the clan of Hibernian Indians, declares that he is not anxious to dispose of Sockalexis, but will keep thirsty Sock on the Cleveland roster till he has accumulated good sense or till Sock's thirst has abated. Tebeau insists that Sock has scattered his wild oats and is repentant." Some sportswriters even gave Sockalexis the benefit of the doubt: "Much of the stuff written about his dalliance

with grape juice and trysts with pale faced maidens is purely speculation," said *Sporting Life* on August 11. Despite this leeway from
the press corps, Sockalexis had little chance of making a comeback.

The Indian would play again that season, on September 11—a
footnote, really, to a season and career. Cleveland had just lost four
straight to the lowly Washington Senators and was two games
below .500 and a distant twenty-two games behind league-leading
Boston. Sockalexis, though limping noticeably, would play gamely.
He hit the ball safely twice and hard at least three times out of five
chances. His team crushed the Senators that day, 15–4, but few
witnessed the slugfest.

As magnate Robison sat in his owner's box surrounded by a va-
cant sea of bleachers, he thought of what might have been. The
season had started out so promising. He had imagined his team in
September vying for the pennant, his park filled with cranks
rooting on the Indian. He saw Sunday ball thriving in Cleveland,
but the Cleveland courts would rule against Robison's crusade. He
saw himself the envy of his fellow baseball magnates. Now he sat
alone, watching the broken Sockalexis stumble in right field, the
sun setting behind him, the dusk settling on the eerily quiet field.
He wondered how long this torture would last. He wondered how
long he would let it last.

The final baseball game at League Park in 1897 was an exhibition played for the benefit of striking bituminous coal miners in
Ohio. The strike further solidified the United Mine Workers of
America, with union membership increasing tenfold from ten thousand to one hundred thousand members in support of the work

stoppage. For Robison the game was more of a public relations ploy than anything else. As a railroad owner he was solidly on the side of coal mine management.

The Cleveland team was divided into the Indians and the Red Men. The hard-drinking miners seemed to identify with Sockalexis, cheering him heartily each time he strode to the plate. Playing for the Red Men, he went three-for-four and made a spectacular catch in right field. Though he would never again run as he once did, there was no question he could still hit. The only question was whether he would stay sober enough to do it.

A SUBMARINE MINE.

The Naval Court Finds That the Maine Was Blown Up From the Outside.

A Floating Mine Underneath the Port Side Wrecked the United States Warship.

Neither Spain Nor the Spaniards Are Held Responsible for the Tragedy in Havana Harbor.

ALL EFFORTS TO FIX THE BLAME PROVE UNAVAILING.

The Explosion of the Mine Caused the Explosion of the Two Magazines on Board the Maine—Two Explosions, With a Very Short Interval Between Them, Occurred, the Vessel Lifting on the First Explosion— No Blame is Attached to Capt. Sigsbee, His Officers or Any Member of His Crew—Treachery From an Unknown Source Destroyed the United States Battleship and the Gallant Yankee Tars—An Abstract of the Report of the Naval Court of Inquiry, Which is Now in the Hands of the President, and Which, it is Expected, Will be Sent to Congress Today.

WASHINGTON, March 27.—The Associated Press presents herewith a complete abstract of the report of the court of inquiry, which investigated the wrecking of the battleship Maine

Shock
of

LON
Parnell
lean n
Stewar
tell, d
County
the bu
niting
before

T

Two

Two
escape
hour y
the fa
The fi
Kate
caused

1 0

WINTER/SPRING 1898—*Alexander Winton puts an ad in* Scientific American *and sells his first automobile for a price of one thousand dollars. Winton had the previous year tried unsuccessfully to garner national press by driving one of his contraptions from Cleveland to New York. The eight-hundred-mile trip took seventy-eight hours and forty-three minutes of driving time. The Cleveland Telephone Company establishes its headquarters in the First Baptist Church building; the company sells telephones with side cranks and bulky batteries. Cleveland's Westinghouse Electrical Corporation buys Walker Manufacturing Company for $1 million, partly because of a successful patent-infringement lawsuit Westinghouse waged against Walker limiting that company's production. One thousand Clevelanders volunteer for the war against Spain.*

* * * *

ON THE NIGHT OF FEBRUARY 15, 1898, the battleship *Maine* was anchored in Havana Harbor. The sea off Cuba was calm, the air hot and sticky. The night sky was moonless. Just after 9 P.M., a bugler on board sounded taps. The 350 sailors on board found their way to bunks.

177

On shore, in the Cuban capital, city lights burned like land-locked stars. Spain had installed a new governor, and the rumblings of Cuban revolution had been stilled for months. All seemed calm. That night, Charles Sigsbee, the captain of the *Maine*, wrote a letter to his wife. There was no sign of Cuban rebels in the three weeks his ship had been in Cuban waters, he wrote. The trouble in Cuba would be over soon.

"I laid down my pen and listened to the notes of the bugle, which were singularly beautiful in the oppressive stillness of the night," Captain Sigsbee remembered. "I was enclosing my letter in its envelope when the explosion came. It was a bursting, rending, and crashing roar of immense volume, largely metallic in character. It was followed by heavy, ominous metallic sounds. There was a trembling and lurching motion of the vessel, a list to port. The electric lights went out. Then there was intense blackness and smoke."

After the initial explosion, a second followed, much more powerful in force than the first. The bow of the ship splintered in two, erupting in flames. Men and equipment were jettisoned from the deck. Windows in houses along the shoreline shattered. The ship tilted forward, the burning bow sinking below the waterline. In minutes, the whole of the bow, where most of the sleeping quarters were located, was submerged. In all, 266 were killed in the explosion on the *Maine*. For years after, the twisted wreck of the ship remained in Havana Harbor.

Though the subsequent naval investigation never found who was responsible, American newspapers quickly pointed the finger at Spain. Competing publishers like William Randolph Hearst and

Joseph Pulitzer had for months embellished the Cuban revolt to win readers. Credibility in news reporting was the first casualty of the war. Unsubstantiated stories from the island told of "death camps" and "cannibalism" and "torture." Hundreds of newspapermen were sent to Cuba, including Richard Harding Davis, whom Hearst paid the astronomical sum of three thousand dollars a month to be his main war correspondent.

True to his words to Frederic Remington, Hearst did supply the war, or at least had a hand in hurrying it along. For months after the sinking of the *Maine*, Hearst's *Journal* devoted the first eight pages to the story, packed with editorials demanding revenge. Papers across the country followed Hearst's lead. The news coverage had the public screaming for blood. On April 11, bowing to the pressure exerted by Hearst, Teddy Roosevelt, Henry Cabot Lodge, and others, President William McKinley delivered the news to the nation that we were headed toward war. Two weeks later, Congress made it official by declaring war on Spain.

The war would last until August 9 and was never really a contest. Of the 5,462 U.S. casualties, fewer than 400 were battle related. The rest were the result of yellow fever, malaria, and possibly tainted meat supplied to the troops. From its very inception the war was all about the news it generated. During the "rough riders'" now-famous charge up San Juan Hill, Roosevelt was accompanied by two of the nation's foremost newspapermen. Like any good news story, it also had comic relief. One of the commanders of U.S. forces in Cuba was Joseph Wheeler. A Civil War veteran, Wheeler was a couple soldiers short of a full platoon. While addressing his troops, he often called the Spanish army "Yankees." But for three months during the spring and summer of 1898, the United States was awash in patriotic fervor.

On March 1, 1898, with headlines across the country predicting the coming war, the Indians began arriving in Cleveland. Sockalexis came from the east with Crab Burkett and stepped off the train on March 3. He had spent the off-season in Maine, back on the reservation. At the close of the 1897 season he had promised Patsy Tebeau that he would give up drinking. In one news account of the day he had consummated his pledge with a Jesuit priest on Indian Island. Tebeau promised that if the Indian kept his word there would be a spot for him on the 1898 team. From the very beginning of spring training, the manager wondered just how good was the Indian's word.

For Frank Robison, the 1897 season had been fraught with anger and disappointment. It looked as though he had lost the battle of Sunday baseball to the clergy; in August a Cleveland judge had ruled the banning of Sunday baseball as unconstitutional, but the clergy appealed and the case went to the state supreme court. Meanwhile, a double-sided grassroots movement took hold, with the clergy and pro–Sunday ball proponents both collecting names on petitions of those who lived in the vicinity of League Park. On the clergy side, the petition stated that Sunday ball was a negative message sent to Cleveland's youth, while the pro–Sunday ball side said that "baseball played on Sunday is not a nuisance, does not disturb or injure health, conscience or property." While the two sides postured and battled, League Park remained closed on

Sunday. What's more, labor problems, the sagging national economy, and the ineptitude of his team had led to rows of empty bleacher seats at League Park during the week. On top of all of this, Sockalexis, whom Robison had believed to be the savior of his team, turned out to be a drunk and a headache.

But with the coming of spring, the national economic outlook brightened and Robison again turned all of his attention to his baseball team. He even mentioned to the press the possibility of building a new ballpark, complete with a running oval for track and field events. Of course the idea came with the caveat that Sunday ball be allowed. Robison, at least in his public comments, remained optimistic that he would eventually win his battle with the clergy. "I honestly believe that we will demonstrate this season that Sunday ball is a benefit to the city," he told the *Cleveland Plain Dealer*. But there was a more immediate change that signaled Robison's new attitude: Hot Springs.

In the early spring of 1897, the weather in Cleveland had kept the team indoors at the athletic club most of the time. Though the Indians were supposed to take advantage of the world-class indoor track and weight-training facilities that the Cleveland Athletic Club offered, too much of the time dissolved into handball games and steam baths. In Arkansas the team would begin playing ball right away. "Even when the weather is called bad here," a *Plain Dealer* baseball scribe wrote, "it is good enough to let the players get in all the practice they need, and when it is good it is like the most beautiful day that the weather clerk can serve up on Lake Erie's shores in June." Perhaps the magnate thought that the hot dry weather and mineral baths would, as A. G. Spaulding promised ten years earlier, boil the alcohol out of his players. Given the antics of the Indian during 1897, it couldn't hurt.

At 1:15 in the afternoon of Saturday, March 6, the team took a train to St. Louis. There, the following evening, they boarded a "special car" on the Missouri Pacific and Iron Mountain Line to Hot Springs. As steam hissed from the train brakes, Tebeau worriedly walked the platform. All the players had checked in and were seated in the car. All except one. Sockalexis was missing. The *Plain Dealer* described the team's mood: "The members of the team had an anxious look on their faces when the time for starting drew near and Socks did not show up. Tebeau was the most anxious of them all and when the signal for the train was given to go ahead he did not know what to think of the Indian's actions."

At the first stop, in Grafton, Ohio, Tebeau wired the Cleveland baseball office. He requested that Sockalexis be sent along on the 3:30 train to St. Louis. George Muir, the secretary of the team, received the telegram. He waited for Sockalexis to show at the team office until almost three o'clock. Then he hurried to the depot. Again there was no sign of the Indian. The 3:30 train left without the onetime star.

Sockalexis was last seen having dinner Friday night with teammates at the Hawley House, a downtown Cleveland hotel. The *Plain Dealer* reported that at nine o'clock the next evening he again was in that section of the city, "in a down town resort." There he told a local reporter that he planned to leave for St. Louis at noon on Sunday and would be with the team on the train to Hot Springs. Sunday and the train came and went without him. The *Plain Dealer* chronicled the events:

> There was much surprise and regret expressed in all sporting circles yesterday at Sockalexis' actions of the last two days. It was thought that he had completely reformed for the season, but this latest will put him in a very bad position when he has to face President Frank Deh. Robison, who is now in Hot Springs. Despite his declaration on Saturday evening that he would leave Sunday afternoon to join the boys at the Springs, he is still in the city and the indications are that he will remain here a few days longer. It is not a very hard matter to conjecture why he is still in the city. He is short of funds and, as Tebeau took along his transportation with him, it left the Indian in a bad plight and no doubt he is waiting to receive transportation.

In Hot Springs, Robison decided to wait on any action concerning the Indian until the team train arrived and he could speak to his manager. Tebeau liked Sockalexis; he had come to Sock's rescue several times before, as he had considerable influence with the team president. Robison respected Tebeau as a man and a baseball player. But Tebeau was running out of patience. The magnate had long since run out of his.

Meanwhile, the team arrived at its new training camp. Compared to the athletic club and Cleveland's dingy weather, Hot Springs was paradise. The posh Avenue Hotel lodged the team directly across the avenue from the "spring" houses, and its amenities received wide-eyed approval from the players. On checking in, some team members left a nine o'clock wake-up call with the desk clerk. Tebeau overrode the requests, telling the befuddled clerk that seven-thirty was more like it. After breakfast that first morning, the team walked the two miles or so to Whittington Park. Surrounded by majestic mountains and populated by tame deer, the sun-drenched field was about as close to Cleveland as Hawaii. About five hundred or so locals watched the practice, including a significant amount of lady cranks. The fairer of the onlookers wore large light-colored hats and cooled themselves with fans. Some of the ladies of Hot Springs embroidered a banner to give to the team that wins the most practice games.

The mornings were set aside mostly for drills. At noon Tebeau would lead the team in a run back to the hotel. There players would enjoy a dip in the mineral water baths. Some would see the hotel masseurs for a rubdown. Others would just rest in their rooms. The afternoon was set aside for games. For the first few days, these matches were intersquad affairs. Although Tebeau still called the rookie squad the Papooses, the new season's version of veterans was called the Colts. Perhaps the Indian's absence had prompted the change. In the evening when practice was over, the players strolled back to the hotel and took full advantage of the amenities. The *Plain Dealer* described the opulence: "In a few moments the baths are full of ball players. They take a nine-minute dip in the pure hot spring water, a three-minute rub from the attendant, a few breaths in the vapor cells and then lounge in the hot rooms until they have had enough. Another rub and then there is scarcely time to cool off and dress before supper. The rush for the dining room is a swift one."

The sportswriter covering spring training for the *Plain Dealer* that year was Walter M. Robinson. Unlike today's sportswriting that eschews detail and shoves synopses down readers' throats, Robinson wrote in the flowing, unhurried style of the day. Also unlike today's sports scribes, he seemed to be on the players' side:

> There is not the slightest watch kept upon the players after the work is done for they are on honor and have no desire to impede the excellent physical results they are receiving. Some take a bottle of ale before retiring, and some drink it before meals, but that is all the drinking that is being done except a most liberal indulgence in the hot spring water and the men regard as wonderful stuff: Nearly every player has his little folding pocket cup and as they walk along the streets they line up and drink their fill.

Considering that this was the team that had been arrested twice during the prior season, a team that was thought of as one of the most hardscrabble in the league, it's doubtful that their alcohol consumption was limited to "a bottle of ale before retiring." But even if their nights were bacchanalian, their days were spent in nature's rehab. Even the most water-retentive of them could sweat out a keg of suds in those gaseous caverns. The one who needed detoxification the most arrived the second day of practice.

As Sockalexis walked onto the field at Whittington Park, several of the veterans—Burkett, Jack O'Connor, and others—broke from their routine and gathered around him. Despite his lost weekend, he didn't look bad. The *Plain Dealer* reported that he was in "great condition." The team seemed generally relieved. "There is not a man of the old Indians who saw Sockalexis make his splendid start last year but who is pulling hard for him to gather himself together once more and help the team out in its race for high honors," wrote the *Plain Dealer*. Tebeau walked the Indian from the field as the rest of the team watched. Sock would be given another chance, they knew. The manager wouldn't have sent him money for the train to Hot Springs if the team wanted to release him. But the veteran players also knew that Tebeau had decided that this was the Indian's last chance. And, to a man, the veterans wondered if Sock would make it.

Like most alcoholics, Sockalexis had enablers. Tebeau was flooded with numerous telegrams and letters from supposed friends of the Indian saying that the rumors surrounding the events of Sockalexis's lost weekend in Cleveland were false. But the Indian decided to take the higher ground with his captain. As they walked around the confines of Whittington Park, Sockalexis confessed. The *Plain Dealer* recalled the conversation: "I did it again, Cap," he said. "A crowd got hold of me and before I knew it they had loaded me. I had not taken a drop in so long that I did not know my capacity, and before I knew it they had me. I am through for good now. My friends in Cleveland are my worst enemies, I fear, even though they do not want to be. After this I will defy anybody to get me started."

Though the newspaper reported that Tebeau was "delighted to receive the assurance," it was not the first time Sockalexis had made such a promise. As much as Tebeau liked him, the manager had a baseball team to run and outfield positions to fill.

Before the team had left for Hot Springs, Tebeau made a trip to Youngstown, Ohio, to visit an erstwhile outfielder. True to his word, Jimmy McAleer had stayed away from baseball since walking out on the Indians in 1897. His departure, and Sock's drinking and injury, were the primary reasons for the team's disintegration in the second half of the season. Before Tebeau left for Youngstown, a reporter asked him his chances of talking McAleer back into the game. "Oh, I'll land him all right," Tebeau answered. "He can't get way from me. First, I will open up a Saratoga full of inducements and spread them out before him. If he remains obdurate, I will try hypnotism, and I am becoming quite a smooth article in that line. . . . We have got to have him, so that settles it."

As it turned out, McAleer did take the money and, unlike Sockalexis, was ready to go the first day of spring training. With McAleer back on the team there was only one outfield spot not decided: right field. Along with Sock, in competition for the position was veteran Harry Blake and Ollie Pickering, the second-year player picked up by Tebeau from Louisville. In the early days of baseball, with limited use of relief pitchers and pinch hitters, there were only fifteen players to a team. That meant that besides the starting right fielder, the club would bring north only one backup outfielder. Whether he knew it or not, Sockalexis was in the fight of his life for a job. Judging from early spring play, he didn't realize his tenuous position. The writer for the *Plain Dealer* appraised the situation this way:

> There may be an excuse for a fielder dropping a ball, but there is no excuse for his shirking it, and the Indian shirks. He is the only candidate for the right field position who seems to think that the team could not get along without him. Blake and Pickering are working like nailers. The former's fielding is as near perfect as fielding can be and the latter not only fields well but keeps up his good work in getting to base on apparently impossible chances.

But neither Blake nor Pickering could come close to the Indian's prowess at the plate. "When it comes to batting there is no foolishness about Socks," the *Plain Dealer* story allowed. "He continues to land them on the nose and as time goes on and no more whisky glasses get into his batting eye he improves." Despite all of his shortcomings and insecurities, when it came to hitting the baseball, Sockalexis had a swaggering ego. Even with a blistering hangover, it seemed, his eye-hand coordination was magnificent. But this gift was the cause of a great deal of pain. He got away with a lot more than the more ordinary batters. As was always the case in baseball, hitting endears a player to the fans. And Sockalexis was a sucker for ego strokes.

One sportswriter of the day commented on the cranks' adoration of the Indian:

> The public seems to have a grudge against Sockalexis and will never be satisfied until he is driven out of the business. While there are no temptations put in his way here and he has shown no signs of another outbreak, the petting that did him so little good last season has already begun. His every move is "jollied" by the crowds. A scratch hit by Sockalexis is the cause of more applause than a two-bagger by some other man. This would all be very well if it didn't affect Sockalexis, but it does. He is very susceptible to flattery, as Cleveland fans have observed, and it seems to make no difference whether the flattery comes from a few hundred persons at Hot Springs or from thousands on the league circuit. Sockalexis acts like a leading man in a cross-roads theatrical company.

By the third week of spring training, Sockalexis was firmly in third place in the race for the starting right fielder position. The *Plain Dealer* sportswriter handicapping the race wrote:

> If Harry Blake continues to bat as he has been doing for the last day or two there will be no doubt who will play the right field for Cleveland at the opening of the season. In fact, the call would now look to be Blake, Pickering, Sockalexis—Blake by a neck and Pick-

ering a good second. When the Indian tries he is the same old wonder, but nobody can tell when he is likely to try. He seems absolutely indifferent most of the time and nothing seems capable of putting ginger in him.

Something was wrong with Sockalexis. Perhaps he was mourning the loss of his crutch and friend, alcohol; or maybe his booze-soaked cells were still ridding themselves of the poison. Though he seemed lethargic in his quest to make the team, he still displayed some humor. As the rumblings of war were plastered on newspapers throughout the country, Hearst's *Journal* sent telegrams to sports stars across the country asking if they would enlist if the United States went to war against Spain. Cap Anson, prizefighters "Gentleman" Jim Corbett and Bob Fitzsimmons, and several track and field greats all received them. So did Sockalexis. He told a local sportswriter that the only way he would fight was if he were given command of a regiment of Penobscots and the same salary he makes as a ballplayer. He added that his tribe "would be slow putting on the war paint," and that he much preferred a baseball bat to a war club. In the war-hungry mood of the country, his quip was not well received. "Sock's patriotism does not seem to be very warm," the *Plain Dealer* commented.

While Sock seemed listless and unconcerned in Hot Springs, Robison and the other team presidents gathered in St. Louis for the annual league meetings. The heated topic of debate was the rowdy state of the game. In the off-season Robison had proposed legislation that would fine umpires fifty dollars for not sufficiently keeping the games under control. It was ludicrous to place the blame on the poor umps, but Robison's idea was more of a power play and a way to protect the playing style of his team than anything else. Boston's Arthur Soden and Cincinnati's John T. Brush along with other owners were championing rules changes to empower umpires to more easily remove rowdy ballplayers. Robison thought this was a direct attack on his team. Though undoubtedly talented, the Cleveland nine won as many games by pure intimidation as they did by playing better ball.

Robison was much too savvy to go quietly while Soden and Brush back-doored him. Though Robison had more than his share of influence with the league's ownership, this was a battle he couldn't win. Everybody knew the state of the game was out of control. In sports pages across the country, civic-minded wags had shouted the need for change for years.

At the first meeting in St. Louis, the Cincinnati team president presented a report that began: "A measure for the suppression of obscene, indecent and vulgar language upon the ball field . . . to the end that the game may retain its high position as respectable and worthy of the confidence and support of the refined and cultured class of American citizenship." The Indians had to wonder to what game Brush was referring. After a few days of haggling and posturing, the measure was resoundingly passed. A contract was drafted that was to be signed by all players.

The Cleveland team reacted to the rule in typical macho

bravado. When a reporter asked Sockalexis what he thought of the new rule, he replied: "I'll cuss the umpire in Penobscot." Seeing the merit in Sock's approach, Burkett learned a bevy of swears in the Indian's native tongue, Abenaki: *hickehowgo* (robber), *kanylanyee* (green lobster), and several others that were left out of the news report. Jack O'Connor committed to memory a speech, should he feel the need to disagree with a call: "Pardon the intrusion, my dear Mr. Umpire, but do you not agree with me that your decision is a slight injustice? I have no desire to question your ability or fairness, but merely suggest that under some misapprehension you have inadvertently wronged us in a slight degree." Brush's "contract" was sent to the team a few weeks later, and although the players did sign it (some teams refused to), it would have little effect on their style.

Tebeau was at ends trying to figure out the Indian's lack of enthusiasm. With a week to go before the season opener, Tebeau demoted Sockalexis from the veteran squad to the Colts, 1898's version of the previous year's rookie Papooses. The not-so-subtle nudge seemed to work. The *Plain Dealer* noted Sock's change in attitude:

> Sockalexis has taken a brace, or rather he has been given one by Manager Tebeau, and seems at last to have taken a tumble to himself. He has been playing regularly with the vets until the last few days, but has seemed to lack ginger and to have no ambition. All

of a sudden he was dropped from the regular team and put in the right field for the Colts. From that moment a change seemed to come over the spirit of Mr. Sockalexis' dream. He began scampering around after everything that came his way, got the old men to hit balls to him in practice and really began to act as if he hoped to become a baseball player.

Chances are, the Indian's malaise was a by-product of an overwhelming case of self-pity. For a bright flash of a moment, his life was successful beyond his wildest dreams. He was a major league baseball star with national celebrity. He had already made more money that season than perhaps the net income of Indian Island for a year. He had gained entrance, albeit as a curiosity, to swanky hotels and, what was most important to him, the better saloons in cities throughout the country. But if he were to hold on to his star status, the saloons could no longer be a part of his life. As an alcoholic, it seemed too dear a sacrifice.

Still, by the time the Cleveland team readied to break training camp, Sock had shown signs of rounding into the form he displayed at the beginning of the 1897 season. He was also sufficiently contrite: "As to my falling by the wayside," he said to a local scribe, "there is no chance of it. I made a big fool of myself and know it. Mr. Robison and Mr. Tebeau stuck to me longer than I deserved and I mean to repay them. When I get to Cleveland I intend to get a place near the ball grounds to live in and then I will not go down town all the season. My mind is made up and it is no joke. I have a good future as a ball player and only have to take care of myself to keep in the game." His mind might have been made up, but his soul belonged to another master, and no amount of distance or resolve could keep him from its clutches.

Sockalexis was with the team when the train rolled out of Hot Springs heading north toward a new season. He was not, however, the starting right fielder for the opening game in Cincinnati. Despite the Cleveland team's second-half collapse in 1897, hopes for the championship were high in 1898. There was good reason for the enthusiasm. Seemingly unfazed by his long sabbatical, McAleer again looked the steady player he was throughout his career and, with Blake's surprising spring performance, the outfield seemed strong. Robison blamed the prior season's disappointment on the patchwork outfield Tebeau was forced into using. "The loss of McAleer and the fall down of Sockalexis cost us fully," he told a sportswriter. In 1898 the Clevelanders would have bodies to fill in any hole that might unexpectedly arise.

The team was deeper with pitching, too. At the end of spring training, Cy Young pronounced that he never felt better. In the off-season Tebeau had signed a pitching star from the Western League named "Bronco" Jones, and expectations surrounding the new arrival were high. Though Nig Cuppy had broken his arm during the first week in Hot Springs, the cast came off by the last week in March, and he looked to be fully recovered when the team headed north. And the cornerstones of the team that had played for the Temple Cup two years running, Tebeau and Burkett, were still solid. The only question, as the train rumbled out of Hot Springs, was where the Indian fit in the mix.

While the rails clicked by underneath, the Indian sat quietly in the railroad car. Around him, teammates joked and drank. A new season was dawning, and with it came the unbridled enthusiasm of spring. But for Sockalexis what lay ahead was the temptation of Cleveland's night, a place over which he had no control. Perhaps he didn't know that he was headed toward the land of the forgotten ballplayer. Then again, maybe some foreboding feeling within told him that this train was taking him to the end of the line.

ON THE WAY.

Indians Left for Their Train--ing Grounds Yesterday.

THIRTEEN IN THE PARTY

Sockalexis the Only Indian Left Behind.

HE MISSED THE TRAIN.

Hanlon Makes a Big Kick Against the Schedule—According to the A. A. U. Ruling All Athletes Must Register—Cleveland Whist Club Notes —Local L. A. W. Consulate — Running Results and Other Sporting.

There was quite a surprise in store for Manager Tebeau and the rest of the team yesterday afternoon as they started for Hot Springs. All the members of the team that were to leave this city were at the Union depot on time with the exception of Lou Sockalexis. The members of the team had an anxious look on their faces when the time for starting drew near and Socks did not show up. Tebeau was the most anxious of them all and when the signal for the train was given to go ahead he did not know what to think of the Indian's actions.

As soon as the train reached Grafton he telegraphed to this city that Sockalexis was among the missing and that he should be sent on the 3:30 o'clock train in the morning. When the telegram was received a search was made for him. It was then learned that he had not been seen at the

A. H. George, are favorable to the prop and apprehend that there will be no di culty in arranging the match.

WHIST.

Cleveland Whist Club.

The sixth challenge match for the championship badges, played Friday even ing, was won by Arnold Green and A. Horr. The play was exceptionally e throughout, the result being in doubt u the last frame was finished. The score

	Gain.	L
1—Green and A. R. Horr......	7	
2—Stevens and N. T. Horr.....		·
3—McClintock and R. B. Tillinghast		·
4—Williams and Fulkerson.....		·

The regular game at the Clevel Whist club brought out nine pairs. Howells method of progression was u but instead of scoring in accordance the Howells system each deal was av aged and the exact gains and lo credited. In this manner most of the jectionable features of the Howells g are eliminated. The score:

	Gain.	L
1—Hewitt and Salkeld.......	5.75	·
2—Day and Decker	4.50	·
3—Fath and Ellenberger......	1.50	·
4—Bushnell and W. E. Talcott	1.25	·
5—Yesinger and W. A. Gray..	.75	·
6—Baldwyn and C. M. Wilson.	.....	
7—Powers and Forsthauer....	......	
8—Evans and Josephson......	......	
9—Snow and H. H. Wilson....	......	
	13.75	1

The first round in the match game tween teams from the Cleveland W club and the Cleveland Whist club wil played at the rooms of the whist room No. 76 in the city hall buil Wednesday evening, at 7:30 o'c Eighteen deals will be played that even and the hands will be duplicated one w later. The teams will line up as foll

Wheel club, W. A. Gray, captain Gray and Scofield; 2. Mowery and Simm 3. Hanna and Stoddard; 4. Austin Snell; 5. Fontaine and Schleman; 6. l and Weber; 7. Bicknell and Calkins; Fath and Millward; 9, Root and S ner.

Whist club, A. H. Weed, captain Weed and Carleton; 2. Schryver and Talcott; 3. Day and Decker; 4. Bush and Ellenberger; 5. Fulkerson and F Tillinghast; 6, Snow and Stevens; 7. D wyn and Evans; 8. Yesinger and A. Smith; 9. Frost and Williams.

BICYCLING.

The Local L. A. W. Consulate

11

1898–1899—The Treaty of Paris is signed on December 10. No Cuban representatives are invited to the ceremony. Abiding by the terms, Spain begins to withdraw from Cuba, cedes Puerto Rico and Guam to the United States, and the United States pays $20 million for the Philippines. Improvements to the Gatling gun, invented by Richard Jordan Gatling and manufactured in Cleveland's Otis Steel Works, makes it one of the most sought-after weapons in the world; it would remain on the top of the weapons chain for only a decade, however, as the invention of the machine gun makes it obsolete. On July 10, Cleveland's churches hold "Thanksgiving" services to honor the "glorious American victories" in the war against Spain. A Spanish cannon, a trophy from the war, is mounted in Public Square.

* * * *

FRANK ROBISON'S ENTHUSIASM for the 1898 season didn't last long. On April 30 the Ohio State Supreme Court reversed the Cleveland judge's decision and once again Sunday ball was banned. In June, Robison tried to take advantage of the "Leisurely Sunday" vogue of the day. Folks then would flock to parks and beaches, ride bicycles, and even attend theatrical performances on the Sabbath, which not too long before was strictly forbidden. Robison had a construction crew quickly assemble a ball field at Euclid Beach Park where the team would play on Sunday. His thinking was that, among other Sunday activities, no one would bother to enforce the state law. He was wrong. As soon as the mayor of Collinwood, the area in which Euclid Beach Park lay, heard of Robison's plans, he told the *Cleveland Plain Dealer* that if they tried to play a game on Sunday he would have the team arrested. Though Robison groused, there was nothing he could do.

Having lost the battle for Sunday baseball apparently, and with the Indian's career staggering toward baseball oblivion, Frank Robison sulked, plotted, and prayed for an escape from Cleveland. He exerted his considerable influence in the National League to schedule all Sunday games on the road, thereby assuring Robison the visitor's share of the Sabbath gates. The magnate was not a graceful loser. He lashed out often and to anyone who would listen about the insidiousness of the powers aligned against him. He lamented that the Cleveland cranks were ungrateful for all of his effort in fielding a professional franchise. Fans in Cleveland didn't take the magnate's abuse kindly. Despite the fact that the team played well the first month and a half of the season, League Park was one of the loneliest places in town. A bitter labor dispute with workers on Robison's trolley lines further alienated the working-class fans.

Robison's prayers for escape were answered when the great St. Louis showman, saloonkeeper, and baseball magnate Chris Von der Ahe ran out of money. The story of Von der Ahe and his baseball team could fill volumes, and has, including a book by baseball historian J. Thomas Hetrick (*Chris Von der Ahe and the St. Louis Browns*). Von der Ahe's storybook rise in the annals of sports began in 1877 when he invested sixty-five hundred dollars in St. Louis's Sportsman's Park in the hope of attracting a professional baseball team. A German immigrant, Von der Ahe had a circuslike view of how baseball should be presented. Along with serving countless barrels of his beer at the park, he staged fireworks shows and horse races before the games. Players on his teams often complained about navigating the piles of horse manure left in the outfield. Though often ridiculed as a buffoon in the sporting press, his ideas were wildly successful.

As Von der Ahe's baseball enterprise grew, he invested in real estate and other holdings. In turn, he invested his bankroll in player talent. Four times his St. Louis Browns won the American Association title. But the players' revolt in 1891 significantly depleted the ranks of Von der Ahe's Browns, and he took the defections as a personal insult. The year of the revolt, Von der Ahe had Pittsburgh pitcher Mark Baldwin arrested for trying to lure Browns players to the Player's League. Von der Ahe's quixotic attack on Baldwin would be the magnate's downfall.

In 1892 the Browns became part of the National League and promptly finished eleventh in the new twelve-team league. They would go on to lose 640 games from 1892 to 1898. Meanwhile, Baldwin and the Pittsburgh franchise brought charges of their own against Von der Ahe. The ineptitude of the Browns made Sportsman's Park a ghost town. Even the reinstatement of horse

racing, the staging of Wild West shows, and the opening of a wa-
terslide ride called "Shoot the Chutes" didn't draw fans. With
mounting legal fees and skinny takes at the gate, Von der Ahe was
choking on the dust of bankruptcy. If that wasn't enough, Della
Wells Von der Ahe, his wife, was suing him for divorce. The former
Miss Wells charged her husband with abuse and mistreatment that
included refusing her any pocket money, discharging the servants,
and making her do the housework.

During the second game of the 1898 season, Von der Ahe's association with baseball literally went up in smoke. A fire that
started in the bleachers of Sportsman's Park quickly engulfed the
grandstand, the Browns' offices, and Von der Ahe's own residence
above. Seven people were injured and one killed in the blaze. Soon
after the fire, Von der Ahe went to meet a wealthy financier at the
St. Nicholas Hotel in St. Louis who had offered to help Von der
Ahe with his money problems. Instead of the financier, however, a
Pittsburgh detective named Nicholas Bendel apprehended Von der
Ahe and forced him into a waiting carriage, which rode the streets
of St. Louis until a Pittsburgh-bound train was ready to board. At
one point the carriage clattered over a Mississippi River bridge toward East St. Louis. A policeman manning the tollbooth stopped
the carriage. Von der Ahe screamed for help. But the policeman
thought he was joking. The *New York Sun* retold the events:

> Chris managed to climb half way out of the door and would have
> leaped to the ground had it not been for the fact that one of his
> legs was firmly held by the Pittsburgh detectives.

"Help! Murder! They're stealing me! I'm Chris Von der Ahe! Save me!" he yelled as the horses dashed along. When the team neared the East St. Louis end of the bridge a policeman called a halt and ordered the driver to pay toll.

"You can make as much noise as you like," said the policeman to the party in the carriage, "but you mustn't gallop the horses."

"Don't you know me?" shrieked Von der Ahe, wildly. "I'm Chris Von der Ahe and these ruffians in here are stealing me. Help, officer! I'm being dragged out of the state! Save me!"

The policeman, who knew Von der Ahe, and was also aware of the fact that Chris liked to have a good time now and then, laughed heartily at the German's frantic cries, and when Chris repeated his roar for help the "copper" said with a grin:

"Go ahead, driver. Where's he been? To a wine supper? It's a peach, ain't it?"

Whereupon the hack was rattled away to the railroad yards, where Von der Ahe, still yelling for help, was bundled into a train.

With no legal extradition at work, newspapers labeled the event "a kidnapping." Baldwin's attorneys had orchestrated the abduction. Unable to come up with the bond, Von der Ahe was jailed. The next day he was released with the proviso that he make arrangements to have money wired to Pittsburgh to cover the lawsuit. A Pittsburgh paper described the proud magnate in a rumpled state with "buttons torn from his vest and coat." Von der Ahe couldn't come up with the cash and was promptly arrested again. Eventually the National League bailed him out. But his Browns were sold at a sheriff's auction to a consortium run by Frank Robison.

The role the Indian played on the Cleveland team in 1898 was almost nonexistent. When he did play it was mostly as a pinch hitter and fill-in. He started the second game of the season in Cincinnati, but only because Crab Burkett was called back east due to his son's illness. It was almost as though Patsy Tebeau had kept him on the team only because he was so well liked by his teammates. "He's a good fellow," Jack O'Connor once said of Sockalexis. "I never saw him lose his temper, not for even an instant. He's always the same ready and willing man to crack a joke with you." Whether it was his affability or that Tebeau still had some modicum of faith that he would return to his old form, Sock was perhaps the most infrequently played baseballer on a National League roster.

Despite his rare appearances on the diamond, the Indian managed to find his way into print quite often. According to the *Plain Dealer*, on May 7, as the team was heading by train to Cincinnati, Sockalexis walked into the smoking car for a cigar. There he encountered a group of army recruits on their way to deployment in the war against Spain. One of the recruits mistook Sock for a Spaniard, and heated words quickly evolved into a row. "When he started to leave one of the blood thirsty recruits tried to upper-cut the big Indian," the *Plain Dealer* reported. "There was a mix-up and for about five minutes Uncle Sam's new candidates for military honors found in Socks the toughest proposition they ever tackled outside of a Missouri mule. He was simply chock full of fight and when the Rubes gave him the opening he was quick to take advantage of it." By the time Tebeau rushed into the smoking car to come to the Indian's aid, the fight was over, with several of the servicemen nursing their wounds.

On Memorial Day, once again the Indian found himself at New York's Polo Grounds, the site of his biggest achievement as a major leaguer. He didn't start the game but was brought in as a pinch hitter late in the game. Once again, the big crowd rose to its feet and chanted. Once again, Amos Rusie was on the mound. And once again, the Indian rose to the occasion. It wasn't a home run this time but a sharp single to center that scored two runs and silenced the throng. It would be Sock's last appearance in New York. It was also the last time he'd be a hero on the big league baseball diamond.

By July the Cleveland team had begun to move backward in the standings. The Indian would, here and there, get into a game. He played in Chicago on the Fourth of July and was greeted with a shower of firecrackers from the stands. There were stories in the papers of Sockalexis being released or traded. There was also a report that the Indian's vow of sobriety in Hot Springs had lasted only as long as it took the train to arrive in Cleveland. This item ran in a Pittsburgh paper at the end of the 1898 season:

Poor Lo Sockalexis, of the tribe of Penobscot and Tebeau, will probably be placed under the hammer of the fire, smoke and water sale of damaged baseball goods which is to be one of the features of the annual league meeting. Sock swears by his feathers of his ancestors that he hasn't removed the scalp from even one glass of the foamy beer since early last spring, when he whooped up a dance on Superior Street, in Cleveland, and was discovered the next morning by Tebeau in the act of fastening a half-Nelson to a lamppost in front of the Hollenden house. Sock might draw his own salary as a freak feature in the minor league or a wild west show, but the wiles and temptations of the big cities stimulate poor Lo's thirst and set him forth in search of the red paint.

Along with obviously pointing out the prejudice of the day, the article gives some insight as to why Sockalexis remained on the Cleveland team for the 1898 season: no other team wanted him. Regardless of Tebeau's warm personal feelings for the Indian, the manager was still a baseball man. He might be stuck with Sockalexis because of a signed contract, but he wasn't going to chance the team's hopes with Sockalexis as a starter. For the season the Indian would come to bat sixty-seven times and hit a paltry .224.

As the season wore on, the Cleveland team played sloppy, second-division ball and seemed not to care. In one game in late 1898, a ball went through Burkett's legs in the outfield. Instead of chasing after it, the Crab threw down his mitt and walked off the field, allowing three runs to score. The team suffered on the field and at the gate with the Indian out of the lineup for the last half of 1897 and most of 1898. The magic was gone. Sockalexis's injury and continued alcohol abuse had seemingly crippled the hope of the other players.

By the second half of the 1898 season, Robison had had it with Cleveland baseball. His team played on the road for the entire last half of the season. The Cleveland press took to calling the team the Wanderers and the Tramps. As the prison gate slammed shut on Von der Ahe in Pittsburgh, Robison saw a way out of the jail that Cleveland had become for him. Subtly, his tone in the press changed. He was planning what would become one of the many violations that have been perpetrated against baseball cities over the years.

In 1933, Connie Mack, the owner and manager of the Philadelphia Athletics, began selling the stars that had won for him his three straight pennants from 1929 to 1931. Among the players Mack jettisoned off the A's were future Hall of Famers Jimmy Foxx and Lefty Grove. Mack had a history of financial troubles and had once before held a fire sale of players to raise cash. In the mid-teens he had sold most of the stars on his team who had won for him two World Series in three years, and in 1916 his depleted A's lost 117 games.

From 1971 to 1975, Charlie Finley's Oakland A's won five straight AL West titles, and from 1972 to 1974 the team brought him three consecutive World Series wins. But after the A's failed to make the playoffs in 1975, Finley through trade, free agency, and sale got rid of stars like Reggie Jackson, Catfish Hunter, Vida Blue, and others. It would be the early 1980s before the team was again competitive.

Perhaps the most recent wronging of a baseball town came in Miami in 1998. Despite the fact that the Marlins the previous season had become the youngest franchise to win a World Series title, owner Wayne Huizenga began to dismantle the team, claiming that he was losing money. Stars like Al Leiter, Edgar Renteria, and Livan Hernandez were allowed to leave or sent packing.

Though Frank Robison couched his move in mollifying terms like "franchise ball," he committed no less a sin in Cleveland than Mack, Finley, and Huizenga did to their respective cities. Robison's plan was to run two teams: one playing in Cleveland, the other in St. Louis. But they would be far from equal enterprises.

In 1899, in plain sight and under the bright lights of public outrage, Robison marched every Cleveland player who could still field a baseball down Euclid Avenue and onto a St. Louis–bound train. Robison left his brother, Matthew Stanley Robison, to run the remaining team as, in Frank's words, "a side show." Though young Stanley, as he was called, was an affable, easygoing fellow, he came under intense newspaper scrutiny. Frank Robison changed the St. Louis team's name to the obnoxious-sounding Perfectos. He outfitted them in white and blazing red and sent the old Browns uniforms to Cleveland for the Indians—or, as the press started to call them, the What-do-you-call-'ems—to use.

Owning two teams, or "syndicate baseball" as it became known, was not an idea unique to the Robison brothers. Earlier that year, Baltimore owner Harry Von der Horst, and Bridegrooms team president Ferd Abell entered a joint venture with most of the Baltimore team's talent being funneled to New York, the bigger market. In both cases, in Cleveland and in Baltimore, it was immediately clear that the weak sister of the partnerships was to be left to wither and die. Robison did little to disguise these intentions. He had, after all, been threatening to move the team to another city for years. In one rather frank colloquy he told a *Plain Dealer* reporter that Cleveland "did not deserve" a major league baseball team and hinted that the Indians might be better suited for the Western League, or the minor leagues.

Though still the titular head, Robison left the Indians and Cleveland without looking back. Once, when his new manager, "Scrappy" Bill Joyce, asked him to add some starting pitchers to bolster the depleted staff, Robison reportedly said that he wasn't interested in the Indians winning. "Play out the schedule," he told the manager. "That's your job." Surprisingly, such incendiary remarks did not alienate all Cleveland fans. Robison was adroit at manipulating public opinion through the press. Some hardened fans bought his tale of woe: the pretentious, puritanical ministers, the city's stance against the expansion of League Park, and the manipulation of the police by the saloonkeepers.

But if there was some slack given to Robison as he carpetbagged his stars—Tebeau, Nig Cuppy, Cy Young, Burkett et al. to St. Louis—the grace period did not last long. Even before the season started, the Cleveland press began to call the team, among other names, the Misfits and the Leftovers.

The 1899 Cleveland club is still considered the most inept professional team to ever have stepped onto a baseball field. Now filled with has-beens and wannabes, the Cleveland nine lost a staggering 134 of their 154 games; one losing streak stretched to twenty-four games. The club finished eighty-four games behind pennant-winning Brooklyn, a record that might stand forever. Pitcher Jim Hughey led the staff with four victories; he lost thirty games. The starting rotation lost eighty-seven games against only eleven victories. For the season, the entire team hit only twelve home runs, and the season-high winning streak was two, a feat they accomplished only once.

It was somehow fitting that Sockalexis would finish a short and tumultuous career with the worst-ever professional baseball team. His talent and fame swept away in a flash flood of beer and booze, the Indian embodied everything that was wrong with the Cleveland club. His pitiful attempt at a comeback began in late April. He told the *Plain Dealer*: "I will be in right field when the bell rings Friday, and if I feel as I do today, I'll knock the ball over to Lexington Ave." Like most alcoholics at the bottom of the bottle of addiction, he wasn't quite sure how it had gotten so bad. Even when trying to be bold, he knew he had no control over his demons—"if I feel as I do today."

As the 1899 season drew near, the St. Louis edition of the Robison syndicate luxuriated in Hot Springs, Arkansas, while the Cleveland team spent their spring training in frozen Terre Haute, Indiana. Only eight players showed for the first practice. Even "Scrappy" Joyce, who was then under contract with the Giants but was to fill Tebeau's slot as manager, was not wholly convinced it was a position he wanted. To hedge his bet he bought a saloon in St. Louis, "in case things don't work out," he said. As the dry Arkansas heat limbered the Perfectos, snow fell in Indiana. Joyce left for St. Louis to run his saloon when Stanley Robison didn't give him the money he asked for, and Lave Cross, a journeyman third baseman, was named captain and manager. Cross would be the last big league manager for whom Sockalexis would play.

For the sake of sports theater, the Cleveland season began in St. Louis, which welcomed its new ball club with a parade and marching band. Fifteen thousand fans crammed into St. Louis's League Park, built by Robison, and rang in the new baseball era with cowbells and "tally-ho horns." Robison's preseason hype had the fans in a lather. He promised a pennant winner, and the local press agreed. In the opener, St. Louis blasted Cleveland, 10–1, much to the delight of the hometown fans. Flabby from booze and still gimpy on his ankles, Sockalexis wouldn't play. The next day's headline in the *Plain Dealer* read: "The Farce Has Begun." More than a farce, it would be an outright slaughter, and the Indian was about to be led to it.

The home opener was May 1, delayed two days because of weather and scheduling problems. Only two short years before,

Cleveland's League Park was filled with cranks and reporters straining their necks for their first look at the Indian. On this dreary Monday afternoon, only a hundred fans milled around the empty stadium as Sockalexis warmed up. Such was the sparsity of the crowd that derisive shouts echoed throughout the field. And it was not only the Indian's demise or the ineptitude of his teammates that dissuaded fans from coming. Robison had replaced striking workers with scabs on the trolley line that stopped at League Park. Much of Cleveland's working class would not patronize the cars.

The club's record stood at 1–7, the only win a gift from the Louisville Colonels. The *Plain Dealer* summed up that victory: "won a game but it was no fault of their own." With the exception of a then little-known rookie named Honus Wagner, Louisville was almost as lacking in talent as the Indians. The *Plain Dealer* snidely remarked that the hometown team would be competitive in the league if they could play only the Colonels.

Sockalexis did not play the home opener either. Perhaps Cross thought he wasn't ready. As he watched the game from a solitary position on the end of the bench, the Indian looked old. There is a picture of Sockalexis that survives from the 1899 season. His once-smooth matinee idol features are puffy and bloated, like a lonely uncle. There is a certain deadness in his expression, as if his eyes were looking incredulously back to some horrid event. He had secured a spot on the team only as an oddity—a cheap sideshow attraction, an unsure step away, he must have thought, from Buffalo Bill's Wild West show then touring in Louisville. Slipping quickly

away were the tailor-made suits and the white women of Short Vincent. Gone were the cheering crowds and the slaps on the back
from fast friends at the bar. Gone too was the white facade erected
by alcohol.

Surprisingly, game one of the twin bill was well played. The five
hundred or so fans who, when the weather cleared, eventually
arrived at the park witnessed a tight, extra-inning affair, with
Cleveland squeezing out the winning run in the bottom of the four-
teenth. Game two was exciting too, with the score tied into the last
inning. Only a controversial play where a Louisville runner apparently took a shortcut from second to home by disregarding third
base gave the Colonels the victory. With all the discouraging news
from their recent road trip, the team seemed maybe to be underes-
timated. Even the *Plain Dealer* had flattering things to say. Maybe
they weren't *that* bad. The following day, the Indian would get his
chance to contribute.

A doubleheader was scheduled again that Tuesday. In the first
game, with Cleveland down by only a run, Sockalexis was called
on to pinch-hit. Like the not so long ago old days, the few cranks
on hand rose to their feet and in unison serenaded the Indian with
war whoops. So many times before, Sock had come through in just
such situations. His walk to the plate was a slow, labored gait—a
condemned man on his march to the gallows. Deacon Phillips, the
Colonels pitcher, glared at the big Indian as he set for his windup.
Sockalexis had decided to win the game right there.

The swing was still pretty: fast and smooth with a slight upward plane, the veins on his thick wrists bulging. But it hit nothing but air, and the force of it screwed the Indian off balance. Again, Phillips reeled and threw, and again Sockalexis missed. In the microsecond it took for the third pitch to reach the plate, the Indian summoned all his focus. He saw the ball in a slow rotation, just like he always had. He cocked his bat and strode forward in his powerful compact swing. For a moment—the very slightest of moments—the Indian knew he had his pitch. Only when the ball slapped against the catcher's mitt did the finality of his at bat descend on him. The fickle crowd that had just cheered him lustily turned on him in that instant. With his head bowed, Sockalexis limped back to the dugout. His teammates averted their eyes.

On May 9, first-place St. Louis headed back to Cleveland to play the worst team in the league. That afternoon, as Sockalexis slowly walked onto the field at League Park, a brass band from the Cleveland Outing Club struck up a war dance tune. There was an air of hopelessness about the Indian, and the band's serenade served as an absurd accompaniment to his dejected body language. The pain in his ankles was searing, his gate gimpy and unsteady like the stumblebums in the Haymarket. His expression was defeated and confused. Still, inside there was the slightest hope, a glimmer of what he once was, the boy who ran like the wind, the runner of the hunting party with everlasting breath, the young man who flew the bases with feet barely touching the ground. It was fantasy, of course. He could no longer run. Late in the game that day, he plodded from third toward home on a single and was embarrassingly thrown out at the plate.

Cleveland lost the first game of the series 8–1, the second 12–2, and they had two more games to play against St. Louis. Rumors circulated that Sockalexis was to be released; manager Cross denied them. The Indian's departure, however, was only a matter of time. On some level even Sock knew his days as a professional baseball player were numbered. How deeply this must have cut. More than any athletic accomplishment, the defining aspect of his life, the big league, had been his wedge into a society that would never fully accept him. It seemed that alcohol had made Sock forget for a short while that he was an Indian: standing at the bar, his throat whiskey-raw, a cigar and shot glass in hand, the bawdy saloon music and booze-fueled adoring chatter overwhelming the truth. But as the night wore on and the drinks flowed, he'd hear the asides about firewater and the drunken Indian. Eventually as the crowd thinned and the insincere adoration turned mean spirited, he would hear again the drumbeat of truth, distant at first, louder then, finally deafening. More alcohol followed, even mornings, especially morning, when his head throbbed from the rhythmic reminder. But in the searing pain of hangover, the truth would not stay quiet. In those moments, the drumbeat of his past was impossible to deny. No amount of English clothing, no white whore's embrace, and not even the longest home run could change that. And no amount of bourbon could either.

Sockalexis started the third game of the St. Louis series in right field. On the mound for the Perfectos was John Powell, a strapping right-handed power pitcher with a sidewinder delivery. Powell had played for the Indians the year before and had won twenty-three games. Then, still early in his career, Powell was often compared to Cy Young. Indeed, in 1899 he would prove to be one of the best pitchers in the league. For the most part, Cleveland fans were still boycotting League Park. But those who did come to the games were fans of the most rabid variety. In the *Plain Dealer*, Cross complimented the small, loyal contingent, saying that the players should "doff their cap" to the fans each time the team took the field.

Perhaps it was the enthusiasm of the gathering that day at the park that ignited Sock. Maybe it was just a muscle-memory thing, his body for one day forgetting all the punishment it had received. Perhaps it was his way of saying, "I know it's over, but let's not forget what I could once do." As the Indian stepped to the plate in the first inning, the crowd warmly greeted him. He held the bat perfectly still, cocked behind his head. His eyes were focused—a stare that only two years before had formed beads of sweat on the foreheads of the league's best hurlers.

Powell must have had second thoughts. He, like the rest of the league, had heard that the Indian was washed up. Couldn't hold his firewater. Wasn't he just the other night arrested for being drunk in a Cleveland theater? The name of the play was *A New Year's Dream*. That's a laugh; the red man must have thought it was New Year's with the load of whiskey he poured down his throat before the performance. He certainly was dreaming. He was snoring so loud the theater manager called the police to have him removed. What has he to be cocky about? He's lucky he can stand up straight, never mind hold a bat. He won't even see my fastball.

Powell rocked, wound, and let the pitch fly. The Indian saw it as a fastball as soon as it left Powell's fingers. He pulled the old trigger and stepped into the pitch, the bat hitting the ball squarely, right on the Hillerich & Bradsby trademark. The ball was hit so hard that the Perfectos' right fielder, Crab Burkett, had no time to react. If the ball had not been hit right at him—one bounce to his glove—it would have rolled all the way to the wall. Five times that afternoon the Indian stepped to the plate. Five times Powell thought he could throw the ball by him. Five times the Indian hit a rocket. Each time he reached safely.

After the last of his hits, a clean single to right in the ninth, the fans rose and applauded. As the Indian stood on first base, he looked toward his old teammate in right. Burkett grabbed the bill of his cap to salute his friend.

Though Cleveland had a chance to go ahead and win the game in the ninth, the rally would be snuffed out on a spectacular play by the Perfectos' Roady Wallace. The first baseman leapt high in the air to snag a sure bases-clearing double off the bat of Tommy Tucker. Though the loss stung, Sockalexis, for the first time in two years, walked from the field with his head held high, helped along the way by his teammates' slaps on his back.

Sock's last appearance in a major league uniform would come

in Pittsburgh on May 13. Twice in the outfield he fell for no apparent reason. When the cheers directed at him rose to a crescendo, he doffed his hat, oblivious to the sarcasm. The most biting criticism came in the *Pittsburgh Post*, which described his play as "nothing more or less than a tobacco sign in right field. In fact, a tobacco sign could not have done the damage he did." The printed attack did not stop there:

> Standing out in bold relief all by his lonesome, among offenders on this visiting team, was Sockalexis, the Indian. His Socklets must have been heap full of dope, for his efforts to take care of things that wandered into right field were as funny as a cage of monkeys. He was about as fast on his feet as a cow, didn't get within a mile of the drives to his garden and seemed to be dreaming of better days.

Left with no other option, Cross released the Indian on May 17. The *Plain Dealer*, the paper that had once trumpeted the Indian's arrival with the headline "The Great Sockalexis Is Here," documented his departure with a headline that read: "The Last of Poor Sockalexis." The 1899 Cleveland club would stumble its way into baseball lore as the worst team ever. The animosity in this baseball town became so bad that the Robison brothers persuaded the league to rearrange the schedule again; now, instead of just Sunday games, the franchise would play all of its remaining games on the road. Lore has it that after the last game of the season, the Cleveland players gathered in a Cincinnati hotel and gave their traveling secretary a diamond locket because he had the "misfortune of having to watch all of their games."

At about mid-season, St. Louis dropped out of the pennant race. Even with all of Frank Robison's maneuvers, he couldn't orchestrate the nebulous components of baseball chemistry. The Brooklyn Superbas, the amalgam of the Orioles and the Bridegrooms, won the pennant with 101 victories. After the season was over, the National League dropped the four weakest franchises, which included Cleveland. By then Sockalexis had already headed east to find a team that would let him wear its uniform.

sold on Wednesday previous, the cable says
Americans made a clean sweep of all events

Fix Course for Trial Races.

NEW YORK, Dec. 24.— All the trial races
select a defender of the America's cup
ll be held either in Long Island or Block
and sounds. This means that the three
boats that are to battle for the honor
racing against the Shamrock IV will not
seen, all next summer further east than
n and Chickens light vessel, at the en-
nce of Vineyard sound, or nearer New
k waters than City Island.

Holy Cross Athlete Dies.

COLUMBUS, O., Dec. 24.—Lewis Bringard
ner, aged 21, a senior at Holy Cross college
Worcester, Mass., died of erysipelas at th
home of his parents here today. Bringard
ner returned home Sunday for the Christma
vacation apparently in perfect health. H
was a prominent track athlete and last fa
was student manager of the Holy Cross foo
ball team.

SOCKALEXIS, FORMER NAP, DIES SUDDENLY

Indian Who Gained Fame in Baseball Drops Dead in Maine.

LOUIS SOCKALEXIS

BANGOR, Me., Dec. 24.—Louis Sock
alexis, a Penobscot Indian, who wo
fame as a ball player, dropped dea
of heart disease while engaged in
logging operation at Burlington to
day. His body was removed to hi
home in Old Town tonight.

Sockalexis was born forty-on
years ago. His paternal grandfathe
was at one time governor of th
Penobscots and the family was promi
nent in the affairs of the tribe. Loui
was an uncle of Andrew Sockalexis
the Marathon runner.

Like his nephew, Louis Sockalexi
was a natural athlete and was abl
to run 100 yards in ten seconds whe
at his best. He became known as
baseball player, in 1895-6 when h
played centerfield on the Holy Cros
team, his work attracting the atten
tion of the big league scouts. In
1897 he was an outfielder for Cleve
land of the American league. After
wards he played on teams in the
minor leagues of New England.

For some seasons past he had offi
ciated as umpire in local leagues.

Will Admit Women Students.

MADISON, Wis., Dec. 24.—Women stu
dents will be admitted to membership in
the new Ski club to be organized at the
University of Wisconsin early next month. I
was announced today. It is said the pro
posed new club will be the only such organ
ization in this country to have women
members. The International Ski Association
of America already has invited the new club
into its membership.

12

In 1830 the U.S. government, on the insistence of President Andrew Jackson, began a policy of compulsory resettlement of Indian tribes to what would be called Indian Territory. It was a policy that would endure almost fifty years. One of the last Native American groups to be forcibly removed from their lands was a small Minnesota tribe called the Poncas. Primarily agrarian, the Poncas were a threat to no one except to white encroachment. Yet in May 1877, government troops stormed into the Poncas settlement, confiscated all farming tools, rounded up the families, and marched them to Oklahoma and Indian Territory. Many of the tribe died of mistreatment and disease during the thousand-mile journey.

The leader of the Poncas was Chief Standing Bear. He lost his wife and daughter to consumption during the arduous passage. As the soldiers led the tribe into Indian Territory, the chief's twelve-year-old son became gravely sick with malaria, pneumonia, and other infections. When the boy died, Standing Bear made the decision to bring his son back to Minnesota to bury him in his rightful resting place. With thirty followers and a single wagon carrying the boy's body, Standing Bear set out for home.

In many ways, the journey back was harder than the one to Indian Territory. In the dead of winter, with few blankets and little food and in constant fear of government troops, many of the small band of Indians became deathly ill. When they reached the Omaha Reserve south of Minnesota they were arrested by General George Crook and jailed. Crook was a famed Indian fighter who had engaged in legendary battles against Geronimo and the Apache in Arizona.

T. H. Tibbles, a Nebraska newspaperman, heard of the Poncas' plight and wrote about it. With the growing power of the press, the story gained national attention. A group of sympathetic citizens raised money for Standing Bear's release on a writ of habeas corpus. The government refused to exercise the writ, insisting that under the Constitution, an Indian was not a "person within the meaning of the law."

At the trial, Judge Elmer Dundy allowed Standing Bear to speak. The chief's words were so heartfelt and eloquent that many in the courtroom were moved to tears, including Crook and Dundy, who rejected the government's argument and ordered Standing Bear and his followers freed. It is said that Crook himself escorted Standing Bear and his followers back to their land. The chief would become a hero of Native rights, often speaking at eastern-city lecture halls to full houses. His people would eventually return to Minnesota, where some of their descendants live today.

* * * *

THERE IS LITTLE DOCUMENTATION on Sockalexis in the months immediately following his release from Cleveland. It is known that he signed on with a few minor league clubs in Hartford, Connecticut, and Lowell, Massachusetts. But just as he had in the bigs, he drank himself from these leagues too.

In the scattered written history of that period of his life, Sockalexis surfaces again on Patriot's Day in Massachusetts. An article dated April 18, 1900, in the *Holyoke Daily Transcript* announced Sockalexis's arrival on the local baseball scene:

> Baseball cranks will have an opportunity to see a fast game in this city tomorrow afternoon. Arrangements have been made to have the Easthamptons play a picked Holyoke team, made up of several prominent Holyoke players and re-enforced by Sockalexis, the noted Indian fielder for the Cleveland National League team last season. Sockalexis is now in the city and is in fine training for the game.

With the attending publicity, some two thousand fans watched the Patriot's Day game. Though fighter Tom Sharkey doing the umpiring got top billing in pregame advertising (in 1896, Sharkey had won a much-disputed Heavyweight Championship when referee Wyatt Earp disqualified his opponent, Bob Fitzsimmons, for delivering a low blow), Sockalexis garnered most of the attention. When he was announced, the applause and war whoops drowned out all that Sharkey had received.

For most of that summer, Sockalexis drifted from pickup games to semipro leagues. For each appearance he was paid a few dollars, which undoubtedly was spent on liquor. There comes a time in any alcoholic's addiction when the only friend left is the bottle, and the only comfort, drunkenness. In small New England and Pennsylvania towns, with boozed-up acquaintances and fast operators who traded on his dwindled celebrity, Sockalexis was at the bottom of his personal hell.

By the late summer of 1900, Sockalexis was living on the street, begging for money to buy a cheap half-pint. He was fodder for jokes, some of which made their way into print. A Providence, Rhode Island, newspaper of the day quipped: "Curved balls are not the sort of benders that have kept the Redman down." With alcohol fueling the downward spiral, there was no way of stopping the descent. On August 24, 1900, the *Holyoke Daily Transcript* ran this news item:

> Without a friend to help him, this morning in the police court Louis Sockalexis, the once petted and famous Indian ball player, was sentenced to the house of corrections for a month for being a vagrant.
>
> Last Patriot's Day it will be remembered he was the bright star of the game in this city which Sharkey claimed to umpire. He attracted really more notice and applause than Sharkey. Last year he fell from grace and played mostly in Connecticut, going lower and lower because of his dissipated habits. He was a fine player and could draw big crowds for the once or twice to see him and club after club had to release him.
>
> His entrance into the big leagues as a member of the then fa-

mous Cleveland club is well remembered in baseball annals. He was the pet of the town and played fine ball. He was one of the most magnificently built men in the business and the women petted him. He had everything that he could wish for in those days. Prosperity killed him and the lessons in dissipation learned in Cleveland have never been forgotten. He learned those lessons of pleasure too well.

Now he is branded as a vagrant. No decent pawnbroker would give him a cent for his clothes and he has often gone to sleep in a barn without supper and dinner, too.

He was arrested last night for sleeping in barns and being idle arraigned as a vagrant. With the Indian stolidity of face he sat staring at the wall while Clerk Tierney read off the sentence of one month in the house of correction. And there the one-time idol will be for the next month.

Sockalexis is the son of the chief of the Oldtown, Me. Tribe of Indians. He is a full-blooded Indian, one of the very few of this section of the country. His folks and tribe have disowned him because of his actions. At the time Pat Cray was umpiring in the New England League he was the guest of Sockalexis at his home in Oldtown. He had a good home there.

He went through Holy Cross college and has a splendid education, far better than the vast majority of his nationality. He had a fine chance to become a leading man in his section, but he threw it all away.

Unlike King Kelly, Babe Ruth, and later Mickey Mantle, whose alcohol consumption (along with their statistics and longevity) gained for them legendary status, Sockalexis was but, alas, a drunken Indian. It was almost as if the sports and news writers who covered his career shrugged their collective shoulders to say: "What did you expect?" Just as they had clamored to write of his entrance into the National League, they rushed to cover his disgrace. In some ways it was a better story. The stereotype had self-fulfilled.

A few days after the Indian's arrest, a reporter from another local paper visited the Indian in the Holyoke jail. This article from the *Springfield Union* was dated August 26, 1900:

Attired in clothes which no tramp would accept as a gift, and peering out into the big and airy reception hall from behind a massive barred and screened prison door, L. S. Sockalexis, the once famous National League baseball player, told a Union reporter the story of his life and downfall, yesterday. . . .

Drink, the curse of the Red Man, is responsible for the downfall of Sockalexis—the Indian, who for years was the wonder and admiration of baseball cranks. Several times before he has been arrested, but never before has he been compelled to spend more than one night at a time locked up.

He is an exceptionally intelligent-looking man and while in college was a good scholar. . . . His great work as a centerfielder brought him newspaper notoriety such as few ball players have enjoyed and for a while he was equal to the occasion. Everywhere he appeared he won applause. His work with the stick was unparalleled. It was seldom that he didn't score a home-run, or at least a three-bagger, and no matter who was the pitcher, Sockalexis was too much for him and no curves were too puzzling. After joining the National League he at one time led the list in batting and fielding averages.

Away up the Penobscot River in Maine, several miles above Bangor, is situated the quaint old town of Oldtown. Across from the town is an Indian village, famous throughout the country as the home of the remnants of one of the greatest of Eastern tribes, the Penobscots. Every year great numbers of visitors flock to the island. They come away loaded with blankets, bows and arrows and Indian relics. Women manufacture them and women, or squaws as they are called, do what little farm work is necessary. The "braves" beg or act as guides: they do not think it a sign of degeneracy, and they have all grown rich. Few of them are left and those few pupose [*sic*] to enjoy themselves.

It was here that Sockalexis was born and he hopes to return to his home next spring.

When the reporter talked with him yesterday, he was surprised to hear him speak absolutely perfect Englaish [*sic*] without a suspicion of foreign accent.

"O, I've always played ball," began the ex-fielder. "It comes natural, I suppose, like anything else. All the rest of the boys played and so I did.

"When I was a young fellow I went to a Catholic school down in Maine. I wanted an education and I studied hard for it. . . . I was on the school team and played in the field and with all this practice it was only natural for me to know my game.

"Then, when I was old enough, a friend wanted me to go to Holy Cross and play there. They always have a great team, so I was delighted and went to Worcester. There I took a special course in Latin and Greek and played on the '95 and '96 teams.

"In '97 the Cleveland National League team offered me a fine job, and as I like to play so well, I naturally accepted and left college. It was a big jump for an amateur to a National League team, and I was much surprised to get such an offer. I played for them for two years and then they 'farmed' me out to Hartford.

"I was with the Eastern league team for several months and played in Springfield. Then I left and played with the Waterbury (CT) team for a while, but left on account of an injured leg. Since then I have had hard luck and have drank more or less. My mother died in February and now no one is left but my father and myself."

In many ways, Sockalexis was behind bars from the day he left the reservation to play college ball. In the jail in Holyoke he told the reporter that he wanted to go home. In the forced dryness of the cell, he realized that the reservation was the only real home he had ever known. It was on the small confines of Indian Island where he could find what was left of his life.

Over a four-year stretch, from the day he left Holy Cross for Notre Dame to his days of vagrancy in Massachusetts, Sockalexis had been back to Indian Island only a few times. One time he attended the wedding of a close childhood friend. On another occasion he stood at that altar himself, but the vow he took then was not in marriage but a pledge to a Jesuit priest never to touch alcohol again. His promise didn't last. His drinking had separated him from his family and his culture. His relationship with his father was tenuous at best. Even the far-fetched myth, his father's canoe ride to Washington, D.C., had to be based in some truth.

Perhaps the Indian's father had a firmer grasp than his son on the reality of the United States at the turn of the twentieth century. If the quote was correct, and the Indian's father did in fact try to dissuade his son from playing "the white man's game," perhaps he had hoped for something bigger, more encompassing than just baseball. In the confines of the small world of the Penobscot, then around four hundred members of the tribe on Indian Island, the elder Sockalexis saw safety and security. As it had for hundreds of years, the island and the natural mote of the Penobscot River had kept the white man's big-business dealings away. For all of his life, the elder Sockalexis watched young Penobscots leave Indian Island to become nothing more than indentured servants for logging concerns. To him, big league baseball was no different than the logging companies, and his son's talent no different than his fellow tribesmen who were deft at navigating the white water of the Penobscot to drive the logs downriver.

For Sock, baseball was the vehicle out of the smallness of the Penobscot world. The zirconium shimmer of the professional baseball diamond beckoned with false promise. He had seen it as his ticket out, a way to rid himself of the ridiculous feathers of his ancestry. But no matter how many layers of English tweed he wore, he could not change the bronze pigment of his skin. All the courses of Latin and Greek could not quiet the whispered voice of his past.

Less than a month after he was released from jail in Holyoke, the Indian was again arrested for vagrancy, this time in Pittsburgh. In the courtroom he experienced a severe case of delirium tremens. The Pittsburgh paper described the former star as a "sorrowful spectacle" and "suffering from an extreme case of nerves." He was shaking so badly his bones rattled. He was at the point of his alcoholism where his body was violently rejecting the poison.

For the next few years, when he could pull himself together, Sockalexis played ball for the local teams near Hartford. But he spent most of his waking hours drinking. One local newspaper documented his sorry existence: "For the last year or so, Sockalexis has been a hanger-on around the cheap saloons in Hartford and other New England cities."

After a while, Sock drifted back to Maine. One day in Portland, wearing threadbare jeans and an old University of Maine baseball cap, Sockalexis stood in front of a theater. There, several boys from Holy Cross surrounded him. A Portland newspaper recounted the event:

"Look, an Indian," one of them remarked, not recognizing his school's most famous product.

"Yuh, and a college one too," another added, as he snapped the brim of the Indian's hat.

As the young men continued to poke, asking the Indian to give them a war cry and war dance, a large figure approached from across the street. "There isn't one of you fit to carry this fellow's shoes," the muscular man said. "You're looking at the greatest ballplayer who ever lived." With that, "Crab" Burkett, who was then the manager of the Worcester college team, put his arm around the Indian's shoulders and walked his old friend down Congress Street.

The story goes that in 1901, soon after his father died, Sockalexis made his way to Bangor, Maine. One evening, broke and half-drunk, he tried to hop a train at the Bangor station. A railroad man saw him sneaking onboard and hustled him off. A nearby traveler recognized the once-famous baseball star and paid his fare to Old Town. The Indian was going home.

Every now and then over the next decade or so, stories about Sockalexis would appear in papers across the country. It was reported that he worked as a ferryman on the Penobscot. For a short time he had a job with the Colt gun manufacturer in Hartford, but in what capacity is not clear. He worked for a logging company as a lumberjack. Some of the news stories had the Indian "dying in poverty" and "a ghost of his former self." The truth, however, was not quite as dire. Back on Indian Island it seemed he was able to knit together some of the tatters of his life—as if he had given up drinking, or at least drank less frequently. With the glow of Cleveland nightlights dimming in his alcohol-clouded memory, the money from the major league contracts long gone, and the cheers of thousands of baseball cranks quiet for some time, it seemed he had at last found some peace.

According to a written account of the day, each June the Indian would paddle his canoe down the Penobscot River to Castine, Maine. There he would visit his uncle Joe's family and in the early evening, when the air chilled and the surface of the river's inlets broke with pike and bass, Sockalexis and his uncle would search the shoreline for birch bark and clams. The Indian's nephews and nieces would fashion the bark into toy canoes to sell door-to-door to summer residents of Castine. The clams were for family supper.

On Saturdays a baseball game would be played in Castine. On the grounds of an English fort from the Revolution, a baseball diamond lay. The game would feature college players from Yale and Harvard summering in the area with their wealthy families. But the crowd seated shoulder to shoulder on the natural bleachers of the fort's embankments were there for one reason. The former fleet-footed star played first base now—too slow for outfield duty anymore. As his team warmed up he would wow the crowd seated on the ramparts by whipping the ball underhanded, like he was skipping a stone over a pond, all the way across the diamond. The third baseman rarely had to move his glove.

Though slow afoot, at the plate Sockalexis still had his eye and power, often driving the ball over the crowd and into a mote that lay beyond the embankment. In one of these games, a pitcher motioned his catcher away from the plate and began to issue Sockalexis an intentional walk. After two called balls, the third pitch was again aimed well wide of the strike zone. Sockalexis stepped over the plate, flicked the bat, and rifled the ball over the embankment and into the mote.

Even as his life became small, manageable, and in a way serene, the national press still hungered for his story. "Sockalexis, Fat and Lazy, Takes Ease in His Tribe," read the 1912 sports headline in a Philadelphia paper. The story told of Sockalexis's insatiable hunger for sports news, "never misses a line; devours every big league game with a great gusto . . ." The story also chronicled his days of umpiring in the northern reaches of Maine.

The Northern Maine League in the early days of the twentieth century was a notorious cauldron of gambling. The teams were made up of expatriated big leaguers, college stars looking for paychecks, and local legends who, like Sockalexis, had hit the bottle too hard. Owners of the largest potato farms in the state bankrolled the teams, hemorrhaging money for the best players available and waging huge sums on the games. Umpiring these games was a dangerous proposition, with more than one arbiter subjected to bodily harm. The league tried several ex-professional umps. But these men found the position too dangerous.

One league official suggested they try Sockalexis, who had been umpiring county games around Old Town. Sockalexis brought to the position an encyclopedic knowledge of the rules and a quiet dignity that even the most volatile player couldn't ruffle. A Philadelphia sportswriter once wrote of the former big league player's umpiring prowess: "He soon won the confidence of the batteries for his unerring judgment on balls and strikes. He was on top of every base play. He insisted on big league discipline of the players. He said but little, but when he had occasion to express himself to a player he let fly a single bolt of sarcasm that was withering as it was unanswerable."

For Sockalexis, baseball had been, by turns, the cause of his greatest joy and deepest pain. In his years back on Indian Island he had finally found a place where happiness came far from the cheering crowd. Though he was never married and had none of his own, it was in children where Sock finally found peace.

Perhaps the greatest gift baseball handed Sockalexis was his knowledge of the game. Not far from the clearing on the bank of the Penobscot River, the place where he had once watched some college boys play the white man's game, he shared his gift. With a smile that once dazzled the fair maidens of Cleveland still quick as a flick of his bat, Sockalexis gently taught the young Penobscots the nuances of baseball: how to work a walk from the toughest of pitchers, how to hit to the opposite field, and when to try and steal a base. At least five of his players went on to play professional ball in the New England League. All of the young Indians left him knowing how to play the game. "Soc taught us to get on base and not to worry about the extra base hit," one of the Indian's progeny told a newspaper writer. "He showed us all the tricks of working a walk from a pitcher. He told us if a pitch was too hot, just to dunk it. We were proud to play for him, because he could do anything we tried to do—and do it so much better."

The death of Louis Sockalexis was news in New York, Cleveland, Boston, and other major cities. An obituary in the *Sporting News*, January 1, 1914, began:

> The idol of the base ball world 15 years ago and considered one of the greatest players created in the days of his prime, Louis Sockalexis, the Penobscot Indian, is but a memory in base ball's wild eddy. Sockalexis, while bravely fighting years and the exposure of many months of hardship, dropped dead from heart failure as he was engaged in logging at Burlington, outside the limits of Bangor. The stalwart body of the veteran Indian athlete was removed to his home in Oldtown, as thousands of base ball fans and Indians bent low with grief. Sockalexis was regarded second to none when he engaged in the National game, over 15 years back. Mathewson, Cobb, Johnson, Daubert—the entire list of renowns of the present decade can boast nothing over the famous Indian.

Indeed, for years after the Indian died, the hyperbole was spat from the tobacco-stained lips of baseball's old-time greats. Ed Barrow, the onetime Red Sox manager who talked Babe Ruth into giving up pitching and also as Yankee executive helped assemble the famed Murderers' Row of the late 1920s, said that Sockalexis was the greatest outfielder in history. Sockalexis was "the best hitter, the best thrower, the best fielder and also the best drinker," Barrow told sportswriter Grantland Rice.

The old ballplayer was buried in a small, weedy graveyard on Indian Island. His grave was originally marked with a plain white cross, the anonymity a stark contrast to the headlines he once garnered throughout the country. But not even the grave could keep him from grabbing the attention of the sports scribes. According to the *Portland Telegraph*, a Cleveland sportswriter visited Indian Island in 1933 and began a campaign to erect a more fitting memorial for Sockalexis. The following year, with money collected from the tribe, Holy Cross College, and the Cleveland Indians, an ornate headstone with crossed bats under a baseball marked the Indian's grave. The plaque reads:

> IN MEMORY OF LOUIS SOCKALEXIS WHOSE
> ATHLETIC ACHIEVEMENTS WHILE AT HOLY
> CROSS COLLEGE AND LATER WITH THE
> CLEVELAND MAJOR LEAGUE BASEBALL TEAM
> WON FOR HIM NATIONAL FAME.
> BORN OCT. 24, 1871—DIED DEC. 24, 1913
> ERECTED BY HIS FRIENDS.

EPILOGUE

Just before it reaches Old Town, Maine, the Penobscot River splits
in two around Indian Island. There is mystery in the inexorable
flow—a silent witness to forgotten generations. A cement bridge
now connects Old Town with Indian Island. From the bridge, a
rutted road winds through the Penobscot Indian reservation. The
houses along the way are small but well kept; some have 1980s-
vintage aluminum siding. Old Nissans and Toyota pickups are
haphazardly parked on gravel driveways and weedy front lawns.

A hundred yards or so from the bridge is St. Ann's Church. A
newly tarred car park surrounds the small wooden building, and a
sign announcing an AA meeting stands in the parking lot. At the
far end of the island, a large aluminum barn houses the Sockalexis
"high stakes" bingo parlor.

Some modest improvements on the island have come from a
court settlement with the state of Maine. In the mid-1950s a Passamaquoddy Indian named John Peters found in his attic a 1794
treaty between his ancestors and the commonwealth of Massachu-
settes that secured millions of acres of land for the tribes. Along
with the Passamaquoddy, the Penobscots sued the state of Maine

for restitution, claiming that land was taken in direct conflict with federal law. The case went to the U.S. Supreme Court, and in 1980 an $81.5 million settlement was reached. It was then one of the very few instances when a tribe successfully sued the U.S. government for the return of land.

Not far from St. Ann's and cleared from a thicket of woods is the tiny "lower" graveyard where Louis Francis Sockalexis is buried. His grave is some distance back from the road, and overgrown with weeds. Perhaps the most interesting portion of the inscription on the plaque is the omission of any professional team name. It says, THE CLEVELAND MAJOR LEAGUE BASEBALL TEAM.

Whether or not the Cleveland Indians were named after Sockalexis has caused much debate recently. For years the popular tale was this: From 1902 to 1915, the Cleveland team was named the Naps, after star player Napoleon LaJoie. When LaJoie was traded on January 5, 1915, the *Cleveland Plain Dealer* ran a contest for a new team name. The name "Indians" was then suggested by fans, to resurrect the popular time when Sockalexis played for Cleveland. There was, in fact, no contest. After LaJoie's departure, Cleveland team owner Charles W. Somers asked local sportswriters to come up with the new name: "The title of Indians was their choice, it having been one of the names applied to the old National League club of Cleveland many years ago," said the *Plain Dealer* on January 17, 1915. There are those who believe that the name was a knockoff of sorts of Boston's "Braves," a team that in 1914 astounded the baseball world by winning sixty of their last seventy-six games and going from last place on July 4 to win the pennant that year. But it's hard to imagine a bunch of old Cleveland sports-writers coming up with the name "Indians" and not talking at length about Sockalexis.

Whether or not the Cleveland Indians were named after Sockalexis will be argued, I imagine, for some time. So too will the political correctness of the name be debated. No doubt Sock would get a charge out of all the fuss; 105 years after a special Indian summer on the professional baseball diamond there are still news clippings to collect.

ACKNOWLEDGMENTS

There are many who helped with this book; for those I forget to mention, I am truly sorry. The ones who immediately come to mind are Jennifer Marino, who introduced me to the story of Sockalexis and whose initial research gave me a head start; Joseph Orso, whose suggestions and keen reading eye helped immeasurably; Russell "Cappy" Gagnon, the oracle of Notre Dame for all of his help; author and baseball historian Luke Salisbury, whose wonderful fictional account of Sockalexis's life, *The Cleveland Indian: The Legend of King Saturday* (The Smith, 1992), was tremendously insightful and helped immensely; the National Baseball Hall of Fame in Cooperstown and the fabulous staff and resources of the A. Bartlett Giamatti Research Center; also, the archives staff at Holy Cross College, and members of the Society of American Baseball Research, too numerous to mention.

A lion's share of the information about Cleveland came from John Grabowski and *The Encyclopedia of Cleveland History*, compiled by David D. Van Tassel and John J. Grabowski (Indiana University Press, 1996), and William Ganson Rose's *Cleveland: The Making of a City* (Kent State University Press, 1990). I used numerous volumes of Native American histories, including James Wilson's *The Earth Shall Weep* (Grove Press, 1999).

I want to thank Gene McDonald for all his help and support.

I would also like to thank my editor at Rodale, Chris Potash, for his deft and guiding hand, and Rodale's Stephanie Tade for her faith and friendship. As always my love goes to my agent, Jane Dystel, and her faithful sidekick Miriam Goderich. And finally, a long-overdue thank you to Paige Polisner, who as a friend has seen the worst and best of Brian McDonald, and endured both.

ABOUT THE AUTHOR

Brian McDonald is a graduate of Fordham University and the Columbia School of Journalism. His writing has appeared in such publications as the *New York Times*, *Gourmet* magazine, and *Reader's Digest*. His first book, the critically acclaimed *My Father's Gun*, was made into a two-hour documentary that aired on the History Channel in 2002.